Foden

B. S. Watson

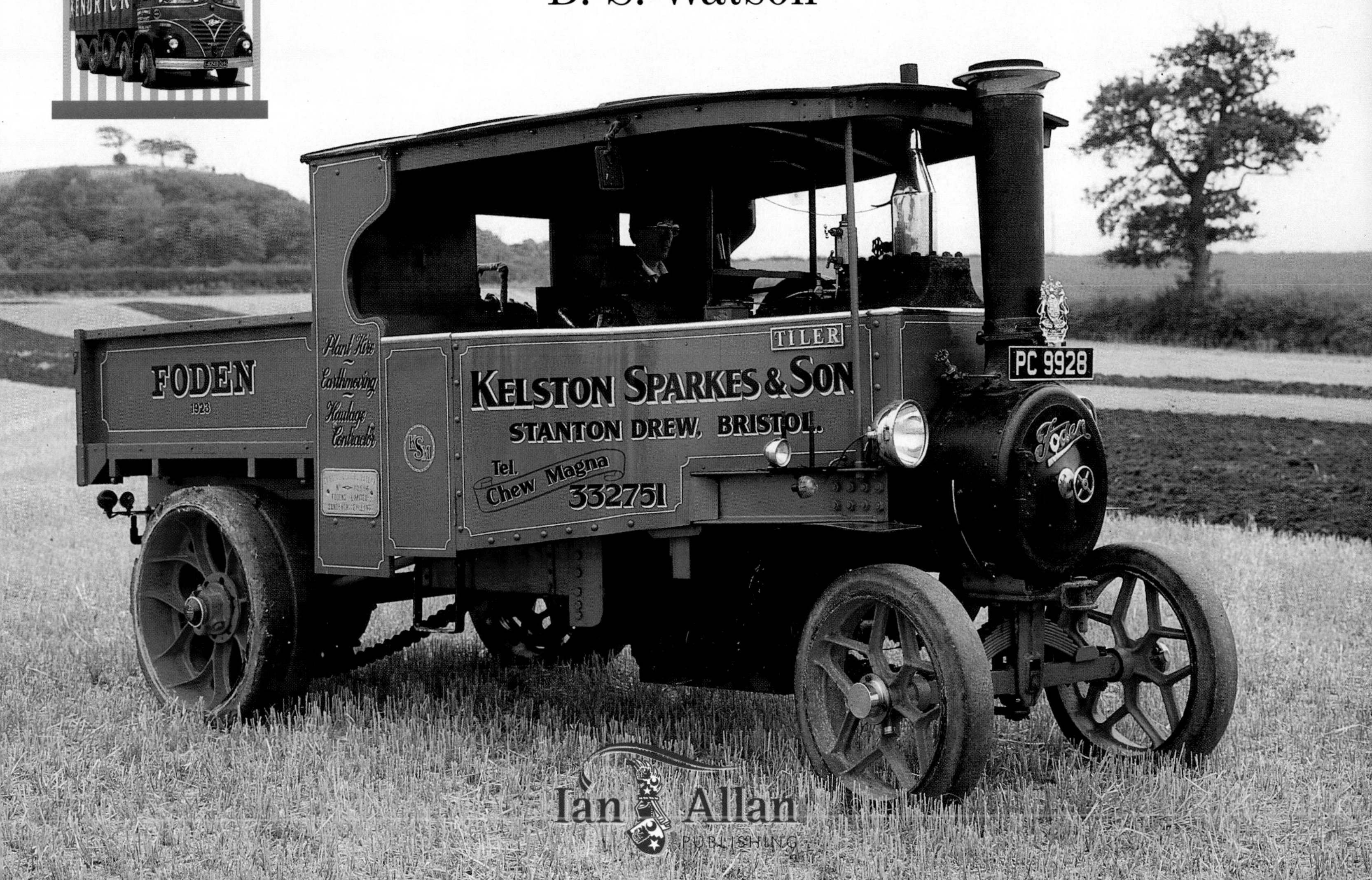

Ian Allan
PUBLISHING

Front cover: Albion Sugar Co Ltd was a regular Fodens customer, and frequently specified enclosed tanker bodies for transporting its loads of brewing sugars and syrups for industrial use. 604 GXV is a 1963 example, fitted with an S20 cab. *Peter Durham*

Back cover: This 1925 6-ton steam wagon (works No 12116) was supplied new to the well-known West Country contractor, W. J. King, of Bishop's Lydeard, near Taunton. Registered TU 1215, it carries a three-way tipper body, and has been beautifully restored from a derelict state. *Peter Durham*

Back cover (inset): The rigid eight-wheel chassis epitomises the Foden marque for many enthusiasts, and 4249 DH, a 1964 tipper, is a classic example. It was delivered new to Horace Kendrick, of Walsall, Staffordshire, in whose colours it has now been restored. *Peter Durham*

Contents

First published 2000

ISBN 0 7110 2733 1

Published by Ian Allan Publishing
an imprint of Ian Allan Publishing Ltd, Terminal House, Shepperton, Surrey TW17 8AS
Printed by Ian Allan Printing Ltd, Riverdene Business Park, Molesey Road, Hersham, Surrey KT12 4RG.

Code: 0010/B1

Title page: Works No 10694 was built in March 1923. Registered PC 9928, it was supplied new to W. Young & Son Ltd of Purley, Surrey. It subsequently passed to an operator in Eltham, South East London, and finished its working life with the Maidenhead Brick & Tile Co Ltd. *Peter Durham*

Left: This striking lorry, seen on test in 1934 or 1935, utilised some cab styling from an SDG6 coach that was built for Whieldon's in 1934, giving it a design that was years ahead of its time. It would appear that it never got beyond the prototype stage. *Ian Allan Library*

Introduction

Writers are advised against the use of clichés, and the words 'the magic of a name' certainly fit into this category. But, for a business that has been in existence for the best part of 150 years, and that has such a long and illustrious history as Foden, the use of these words seems entirely justified. The name is synonymous with innovative design, good quality engineering and customer care and, if you ask any lorry enthusiast to list their favourite manufacturers, then the odds are that Foden will appear at, or near, the top of their list.

Fodens have always had a special magic for me, dating back to my childhood when I became the proud owner of a Dinky Supertoy eight-wheel Foden DG flat truck, and was able to watch the Shipstones Star Brewery fleet running from the brewery at Basford, Nottingham, close to where I was brought up.

In the following years my interest and knowledge in road transport grew, and with it my respect for Fodens. Taking an especial interest in all that they did, I began to consider that I had quite a good understanding of all that had happened at Elworth. Just how naïve I had been in making this assumption I realised shortly after I accepted the invitation to write this volume and began my more detailed research. The sheer magnitude of the material and information that I uncovered soon made me realise how little I actually knew.

One outcome of my investigations was the gain of an even greater respect for the company. A factor that soon became clear is how often those who were in charge of the company had, over the years, demonstrated a remarkable flair for what is now known as 'lateral thinking', both in solving new and existing problems, and in new product development. Whilst managing to achieve the balancing act of meeting legislative requirements and customer needs, they succeeded in building a tremendous customer loyalty by providing only the very best, in terms of product and back-up service.

To condense this fascinating history into a volume of this size has been no easy task, one of my main problems being not what to include, but what to omit, if I were to stay within the publisher's requirements. If someone's 'personal favourite' has been left out then I apologise now. What I have tried to do, to the best of my ability, is to chronicle the history of the company, in an easily-readable, well-illustrated format that can be readily assimilated by the average enthusiast lacking either the time, or the inclination, to become heavily involved in statistics and detailed specifications, but who would like to learn more, in general terms, about Foden.

Choosing suitable illustrations has been one of my main problems, as such a diversity of types has been produced over the years. The emphasis is on working vehicles, but a selection of some of the excellent preserved examples that can be seen at rallies has been included, not just to illustrate particular models, but to acknowledge the great service given to us all by those people who spend so much time, money and effort on keeping the Foden tradition alive.

Wherever possible, facts have been checked to the company's records and the contemporary technical press. Whilst I discovered much that was unknown to me before I started this work, it may well be that there is much more out there waiting to be unearthed by future chroniclers. My narrative ends with the takeover by Paccar as I suspect that, to many enthusiasts, that is where their interest wanes.

As at the time of writing this manuscript it had just been announced that assembly of Foden trucks was to be transferred to the Leyland assembly plant near Preston, where they will be built alongside Leyland and DAF models, thus ending the Elworth tradition. It, therefore, seems an opportune time to present this volume as a tribute to both the Foden family and the Elworth workforce who, working together over the years, gave us so much of which to be proud.

I trust that this volume will be read and appreciated not only by all devotees of Foden but also by those whose interests are more diverse and if, in reading it, they enjoy it and, perhaps, learn something about Foden that they didn't know before, then my task will have been worthwhile.

I must place on record my appreciation for help given by others in the preparation of this work. This includes the Cheshire County Archive, where the Foden company records are held, Glen McBirnie, Tony Peacock and Richard Parkinson, for the provision of some photographs, and all those members of the Foden Society who have given their time and knowledge so freely, and always in such a friendly manner. In particular I must thank John Sanderson for passing on some of his knowledge and also allowing me access to his extensive photographic library, and Peter Tulloch, who again allowed access both to his records and his unrivalled knowledge of Foden buses. I also acknowledge the information given in the previously-published book by Harold Nancollis on the company, which has been useful as a source of checking the accuracy of the facts that I had already gathered.

Barry S. Watson ACIB
April 2000

◄ As supplier of steam vehicles to the Royal Estates, Fodens was entitled to display the Royal Warrant. This could be seen mounted and proudly displayed on many steamers, as in this example. *Author*

1. Historical Background

This story starts in the early years of Queen Victoria's reign. At about this time population growth in Great Britain became an important factor, the population of England, Scotland and Wales doubling in the 50 years 1801-51. This put pressure on the agricultural industry to produce more food, and mechanisation of processes began to be seen as the way forward.

Britannia ruled not only the waves but also vast tracts of the globe, and the nation's industries dominated world markets. To meet the growing demand for manufactured goods, industry began to mechanise itself, and there was a population shift from the country to the towns and cities where the factories were located. A way of life that had changed little since the Middle Ages was about to be transformed to the factory system. The steam engine was the power source that helped bring about all this change, and manufacturers all over the country were striving to produce improved designs.

Transport between major centres of population was virtually the preserve of the railways, whose network was expanding at the expense of the canals that had lost much trade. The road system, outside the towns and cities, was in a deplorable state, and punitive Government legislation had done little to encourage the development and use of mechanically-propelled vehicles.

It was into this world that Edwin Foden started out on his engineering apprenticeship. He had been born into a staunchly Methodist household with a strong family loyalty; this loyalty was, in later years, to extend to a personal interest in his workforce, with a strong concern for their welfare, verging almost on paternalism, that was not usual for the Victorian era.

This is not, therefore, a mere narrative about machines and vehicles, but an account also of the people responsible for the development and manufacture of those products — people who were strong, not necessarily in the physical sense, but in their inner strengths that made them keep going when all around were problems, opposition, competition and ever-changing legislation. This strength of character was called into play more than once in the company's history when it came close to collapse, but each time disaster was averted. This was vital not only for the Foden family but also to their workers and the whole of Elworth and Sandbach, the fortunes of which small Cheshire communities were inextricably bound up with the performance of Fodens.

The company's history started in steam days, building portable steam engines, threshing machines and agricultural machinery and soon moved on to traction engines. Edwin perfected a compound engine and, after an interlude building stationary engines for industrial use, he turned his attention to self-propelled steam wagons, being convinced that this was the way forward. The success of their entry in the 1901 War Office trials provided a catalyst for development, and the company settled down to producing a range of wagons that were successively developed and improved to become widely regarded as the definitive overtype steam wagon (ie where the engine is mounted on top of the boiler). By the 1920s they had no equal, and gave Fodens an enviable reputation.

By the late 1920s the world was beginning to change more rapidly, and overtype wagons started to appear dated. There then began a time of turmoil and uncertainty for Fodens, with competition from the modern Sentinel steam designs and also a new usurper in the form of the compression-ignition — or diesel — engine. Which way to turn was the problem facing Fodens' board and they opted in favour of steam, authorising production of a range of modern steam lorries. These came too late, however, as the days of steam power for road haulage were waning fast.

Even the strong marque-loyalty that Fodens had built up could not save the company from upheaval and near-disaster, for it was unprepared with diesel replacements, and these were what customers desperately wanted — and could already get from other manufacturers. In the midst of boardroom wrangling, one member of the Foden family left the company and moved on to set up ERF. It took the return of William Foden from Australia, where he had retired, literally to pull the company back from the brink, for without his timely arrival there is little doubt that it would have foundered. Fortunately he brought with him a sound, common-sense approach, and a range of diesel lorries was developed, evolving by the late 1930s into the DG series — a range which soon found operator favour, becoming almost a legend.

With the outbreak of World War 2 production became diversified, army lorries, cannon shells and tanks being built at Elworth. Following the return to peace there was an insatiable demand for new vehicles, and Fodens excelled itself, producing a new and improved range of lorries, a revolutionary two-stroke engine, and a modernistic range of bus and coach chassis. All of these were eagerly acclaimed in the drab postwar world that was hungry for new designs.

Throughout the next 30 years there was a continual push forward with new ideas: tilt cabs, glass-fibre cabs, dumper trucks, mobile crane chassis, airfield refuellers and modern army lorries. The company invested heavily in building one of the world's most modern lorry production lines, and made a re-entry into the bus market with an up-to-the-minute rear-engined double-deck design.

Sadly, although there was considerable optimism, the company struggled and, in 1980, the receivers were called in. By the autumn of that year Fodens ceased to be British-owned when it passed to Paccar, of the USA, which retained the Foden name which is still used on its range. But to the writer — and, I suspect, to many others — nothing will ever be quite the same again.

2. Formative Years: 1841-76

On 5 August 1841 Edwin Foden was born in the Cheshire hamlet of Smallwood. He was destined to become one of that great breed of supremely confident and inventive Victorian engineers, and his surname, together with that of the nearby village of Elworth, was set to become well known and highly respected in the, as yet to be created, world of commercial-vehicle manufacture.

Whilst all this was in the future it was soon evident that Edwin had a good practical brain and, with a view to his putting this to good use, he became an engineering apprentice at the age of 15, joining the firm of Plant & Hancock at the Elworth foundry, approximately 3 miles from the family home. This agricultural engineering business produced portable steam engines and threshing machines for the local farming community, and, at times, when work became slack, did sub-contract work for the railway engineering workshops at nearby Crewe.

In view of the way in which Edwin's career was later to develop, it is interesting to note that the father of one of the partners was Walter Hancock, who had been one of the most successful early steam engineers, having developed and operated a number of self-propelled steam carriages in London in the 1830s.

Edwin soon proved that he had a natural aptitude for engineering, and fortune ensured that he was in the right place at the right time, entering an industry where rapid changes were being wrought, transforming and accelerating the ways in which men earned their livings by mechanising more and more tasks. Such was Edwin's enthusiasm and ability for his work that he was appointed workshop foreman at the age of 19.

By all accounts George Hancock and Edwin got along well so it is surprising to find that at one stage Edwin left the Elworth foundry, taking employment in the Crewe railway workshops. Whether this was due to an inner confidence in his own ability, or a desire to progress faster in his chosen career, we shall never know. Certainly he would have increased his engineering knowledge and this probably heightened his desire to run his own business, subsequent events proving that he had a flair in this direction. He was obviously respected, because it was not long before he was asked if he would return to the foundry as a partner, his name becoming part of the business title. At that time the works was building stationary steam powerplants for use in mills and collieries, in addition to its agricultural work.

These were busy years for Edwin, for in addition to being heavily involved in the business, he found time to get married, and his first son, William, was born in 1868, followed by Edwin Richard in 1870. Both were later destined to make names for themselves in the transport world.

George Hancock was older than Edwin and he left the business, initially being retained on a consultancy basis, before retiring fully in 1876. It was not long afterwards that the company was renamed Edwin Foden & Son, in anticipation of young William following in his father's footsteps. The foundations of the Foden family business had been laid.

3. Stationary Engines, Compounding and Steam Traction: 1877-95

The Elworth works had plenty of work in hand at the start of this period and, whilst the workforce was kept busy, Edwin turned his creative talents in new directions, looking at ways of expanding the product range and making its steam engines more economical.

At the time, most engines were of the single-cylinder, simple-expansion type, in which the steam, once it had driven the piston for one stroke, was released by the exhaust valve into the atmosphere. This was both wasteful and expensive as the steam still had some expansive power left within it and was, therefore, capable of providing further power to the engine. The answer to its more efficient use lay in compounding, a system utilising two cylinders and where the same volume of steam is used twice. It is first admitted to the smaller, high-pressure cylinder, driving the piston for one stroke, then passing to the low-pressure cylinder where it continues to expand, driving that piston for one stroke before being exhausted from the engine. In this way coal is used more economically, whilst power output is increased by approximately 70% compared to a single-cylinder engine. Economy of operation was just as important then as now, and would be of even more benefit to operators if a self-propelled engine could be developed that would have to carry its own fuel supply. Whilst this was still some way in the future, perfection of the compound engine continued to occupy Edwin's thoughts.

The agricultural products of the business had a good reputation for being soundly engineered, but even here there was a degree of innovation with the designing of a threshing machine powered by its own, in-built, steam engine. The farming community was notoriously cautious in accepting new ideas, so Foden's success was worthy of note, although helped by successes at agricultural shows and trials. This same means was later used with some effectiveness when Edwin began to market his traction engines.

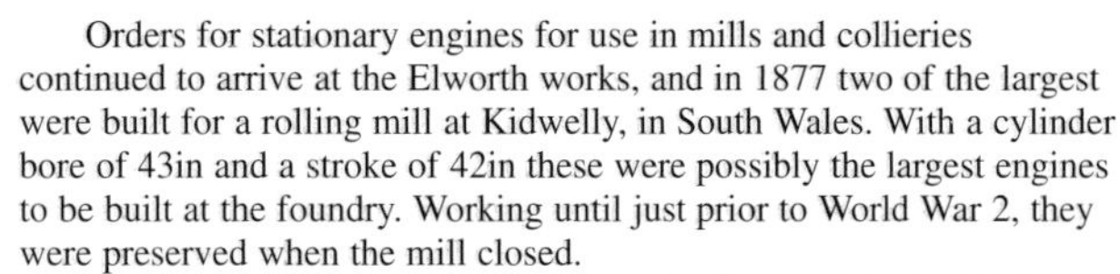

Orders for stationary engines for use in mills and collieries continued to arrive at the Elworth works, and in 1877 two of the largest were built for a rolling mill at Kidwelly, in South Wales. With a cylinder bore of 43in and a stroke of 42in these were possibly the largest engines to be built at the foundry. Working until just prior to World War 2, they were preserved when the mill closed.

During the 1880s the Government gradually eased the legislation restricting the movement of agricultural steam engines on the highway. Whether this influenced Edwin's thoughts as to the future is not known, but in 1883 he exhibited a traction engine at the York Royal Show that featured a sprung rear axle. This design feature had a Royal Letters Patent, entitling him to display the Royal Coat of Arms. In 1887 a compound traction engine won a gold medal at some trials at Newcastle-upon-Tyne, this being achieved in the face of competition from many well-established traction-engine builders. This triumph ensured a growing order book.

Success was not without its problems, however, Edwin realising that new capital was required to finance the purchase and installation of new machinery to enable production to be increased. To meet this need a new company was formed in 1887 — Edwin Foden Sons & Co Ltd — his second son having now joined the business.

A further example of Edwin's diversification at about this time was a venture into marine-engine production, which gave more experience with compound engines. Several steam road locomotives were also built for travelling showmen, although Foden's future was to lie elsewhere.

Edwin had realised, with an extraordinary degree of foresight, that the future for road haulage lay not in the accepted arrangement of an engine pulling one or more trailers, but in the form of a self-propelled wagon, capable of carrying its own fuel in addition to its load. He may have been influenced by two factors. Firstly, he would have witnessed the increasing improvements to the country's roads brought about by the adoption of McAdam's and Telford's surface-sealing methods. Secondly, there was further relaxation of legislation relating to the movement of mechanically-propelled vehicles on roads, which was to signal the end of the railways' monopoly of freight movement.

4. Steam Wagon Genesis: 1896-1904

Marking the start of this period was one of the UK's most historic pieces of road-transport legislation: the Locomotives on Highways Act, 1896. This repealed the infamous Red Flag Act which had required a man carrying a red flag to walk in front of any mechanically-propelled vehicle that was running on a public highway. The new Act allowed any vehicle of under 3 tons unladen weight to travel at up to 12mph unfettered by this restriction.

The new legislation provided the incentive that the Fodens needed to further their steam wagon aims. The future for such a vehicle looked brighter and the father-and-sons team started work on their designs. There were some parameters within which they had to work, the most obvious being the 3-ton weight limit, whilst legislation dictated the size of the wheels, which was related to the load that they would be required to carry. In this respect the Fodens had decided on a 3-ton payload and had further resolved that the wagon must be powered by a compound engine of their own design. In all other aspects of the design there were no set precedents.

The Fodens were actually part of a small group of pioneers, for there were others in the country working towards the same goal, with none of them knowing the best way to proceed. Should the boiler be horizontal or vertical? Should it be parallel with, or across, the frame? What should be its location? Which axle should be driven? Which wheels should steer? They set to work and between 1898 and 1899 produced three working prototype wagons. Interestingly, and in contrast to where Fodens' later success with locomotive-boilered wagons was to lie, the first machine had a vertical boiler mounted at the front of the frame, with rear-wheel steering. A similar layout had been used by Thornycroft on a steam van in 1896 with some degree of success.

The first vehicle did not perform as well as was expected, and also proved to be awkward to load to ensure even weight distribution, so a second prototype was constructed. This utilised a front-mounted, horizontal, locomotive-type boiler, with power transmitted to the rear wheels via friction-wheel-reduction gearing and chain to the back axle. The friction gearing was replaced on the third design by a long drive-chain running from the boiler-mounted engine to the rear axle, which worked more efficiently. This layout became the company's basic design and, with updating, was to serve it well for the next 25 years.

The third wagon (works No 514) was completed towards the end of 1899, and not long afterwards an event occurred that gave a boost to the Fodens' ambitions. This was the announcement by the War Office in 1900 of its intention to hold some proving trials the following year to evaluate the use of lorries for the Army. The Boer War was being fought at this time, and patriotic fervour ensured that the public would follow such an event with interest. Edwin was well aware of the publicity that could be gained by success at such a contest, and decided to enter.

New ideas were included in the third prototype, with the performance of all components being calculated prior to incorporation instead of being built and tested in use. Whilst this is normal practice today it was probably not usual at that time, although it proved beneficial, resulting in a completed wagon that ran very well.

Interestingly, the first wagons were built approximately two thirds of full size. The fourth prototype (No 524) was built full-size, and was to be the actual entry for the trials. It featured an economical compound

The wagon that Fodens entered in the 1901 War Office Trials was a very purposeful-looking machine, the layout of which was to form the basis of the company's wagon designs for many years. Its massive construction is evident from this illustration, in particular the rear axle-spring mounting. The disc-type wheels were soon replaced on production models by the more conventional spoked type. *Ian Allan Library*

engine, driving through a two-speed transmission to a massive rear axle assembly with the springs mounted on the outside of the frame. A clever feature of the design enabled both cylinders to run on high-pressure steam in the event of the wagon's encountering heavy going, while, if a fault arose, it was possible to shut down the defective cylinder and run the engine on the remaining one. The wagon proved well able to carry the intended 3-ton payload.

The trials were to be held in Hampshire, commencing Thursday 5 December 1901, resulting in a journey of more than 150 miles for the Fodens from their Elworth works. The tests were designed to replicate the conditions in which an army machine could be expected to perform, including road running (some of it at sustained high speeds), hill-climbing proficiency, the ability to run for 48 hours without overhaul or cleaning, cross-country competence, and load-carrying capability, including the towing of a 2-ton trailer.

Out of a total of 11 entries (one of which was petrol-powered) provided by various manufacturers, some didn't even turn up at the start, but from a very early stage it became evident that there were only two serious contenders — the Foden and the Thornycroft. The Foden entry performed well, being particularly economical, burning far less coal than its nearest competitors. Unfortunately, the judges favoured the superior load-space provided by the Thornycroft design, which, coupled with its better performance on soft ground, gave it the edge and the resulting first prize.

Despite its impressive performance, several factors had weighed against the Foden. One of these was the poor forward vision for the driver over the boiler-mounted engine, whilst problems had also arisen with the tandem-drive chains, which were virtually impossible to maintain in equal tension. Unfortunately, at that time no single-roller chain had been produced that was strong enough on its own for the job.

The War Office agreed to exercise its option to buy the Foden wagon for further appraisal, and the Fodens were awarded the second prize of £250. They were well pleased, particularly as the newspaper reports had consistently praised their wagon's economy of operation, and knew that this factor alone would bring them orders. The conclusion of the War Office was that the wagons had proved their ability to do all that

This steam wagon has been built in the style of the 1901 War Office Trials wagon, with the massive rear axle spring assembly resembling that of a railway wagon, the springs being mounted outside the wheels. The vehicle is older than 1905 as the design was changed at that time. The bus-cum-brake type of body is unusual, while it is interesting to note that the water tank is missing from its usual position at the rear of the chassis frame.
Ian Allan Library

was asked of them, and far more quickly than could have been done with horses, giving a tremendous boost to the infant road transport industry, in which Fodens was destined to play a major role.

Whether this could have been foreseen by Edwin we shall never know, but we do know that, whilst he was principally a 'hands-on' engineer, he was astute enough to realise that many excellent businesses had failed through a lack of capital and what would nowadays be called a weak management structure. He was determined that this would not happen to his business. A group of directors were brought together combining monetary, commercial and engineering skills, capital was raised, and a limited-liability company — Fodens Ltd — was born in 1902. The capital was soon utilised in meeting the needs of a growing order-book; the foundry size was increased, new workshops and an office block were built and the first wagon was sold to a commercial user in March of that year.

It is, perhaps, appropriate at this stage to make some reference to the workforce and Edwin's relationship with his men, for without their co-operation none of this growth would have been possible. Over the years he had built up respect based on his own ability to do any job in the works with a competence equal to that of his most skilled men. These days, when all too frequently management is from a distance, it is hard to visualise the 'boss' getting his hands dirty to illustrate a point, or to demonstrate to an apprentice just how a job should be done. But that is what Edwin did, and it achieved results in terms of performance, loyalty and respect. The workforce took more pride in what they did, and standards were consistently high, leading to excellent build-quality which, in turn, generated repeat orders.

In these early years Edwin made every effort to get to know his workers by name and displayed a concern for their welfare, sometimes personally visiting sick men at home, setting up a welfare department and social club and establishing a rented housing scheme using properties owned by the company. And, of course, there was the brass band, salvaged in 1902 from the remnants of the Elworth silver band and destined to become one of the best respected and well-known names in brass-band circles.

As for his customers, Edwin was convinced that only the very best was good enough for them, and to this end the 3-ton wagon was modified to improve performance and reliability still further. Whilst traction engines and road locomotives were to be built for several more years, Edwin's main interest obviously lay with the steam wagon, and the company was now set to steam ahead into what was to become one of the most successful and exciting chapters in its history.

5. Steam Wagons Supreme: 1905-24

Not surprisingly, very few early steam wagons survived into the preservation era. This 5-ton example, works No 848, dating from 1904 is, therefore, all the more noteworthy. Although registered in Gloucestershire, it is believed to have been supplied new to an operator in North Devon before moving to the Gloucester area. A temporary extension chimney has been fitted to assist in steam raising, and to keep any smoke well above the heads of spectators, at a Birmingham Science Museum rally in 1964. *Author*

The road-haulage industry — vehicle manufacturers and operators alike —received a tremendous boost with the passing of the 1904 Heavy Motor Car Order, which came into force in January 1905. This permitted an increase in the unladen weight of a lorry to 5 tons maximum, whilst at the same time increasing gross trailer weights, allowing a combined wagon and trailer gross weight of 20 tons. A further benefit was that, if axle loadings were met, and either solid or pneumatic tyres were fitted, then the legal speed limit was raised to 12mph for a solo wagon.

Work was quickly put in hand to modify the current wagon design to take advantage of the new legislation. The basic overtype layout was retained, but the massive rear axle assembly was changed by bringing the chassis frames inside the rear wheels, with the springs held by frame-mounted brackets, the torque on the rear axle being taken by radius rods. New wheels were designed and the body load area was increased. This 5-tonner was an immediate success, well loved by operators at home and abroad, being reliable and cheap to operate, and order books stayed full. From about 1910 the distinctive cast-steel wheels, with Y-shaped spokes and solid rubber tyres, became a standard fitting.

A service to customers that was initiated at about this time was the refurbishment and modification of their existing older wagons, to bring them into line with changed legislation. Whilst this must have done much to increase customer loyalty it can hardly have done much in the short term to boost the sale of new wagons. Despite this, and also in the face of increasing competition from other manufacturers, this was a flourishing period for the company. Shareholders had the benefit of healthy dividends, and the gross profit for the year ended 1910 was nearly £40,000.

Sadly, on 31 August 1911, Edwin Foden died. Whilst he had not been in the best of health for some time, his passing was a loss, not just to his family and personal friends but to the workforce and the whole community of Elworth. There were those who felt that

One of Fodens' products built especially for a travelling showman was 'Prospector', a 1910 steam road locomotive nominally of 8hp. Registered in the West Riding of Yorkshire as WR 6985, it was built for Walter Shaw of Sheffield, and was used to haul a set of steam swing-boats. It has now been preserved. *Eric Sawford*

A survivor from Fodens' early days is SN 1609, a 1906 double-crank compound engine named 'The Pride of Leven'. It is believed to have been exhibited at the Highland Show in Scotland before being purchased for use on general agricultural work there. It was bought back by Fodens in 1956 and was restored in time for the company's centenary celebrations that year, being shown in the parade of vehicles.
Ian Allan Library

the void left by his death would never be filled, but the business had to continue; his sons, William and Edwin Richard — both now in their early forties — had learnt it well and took to the task of moving the company forward with enthusiasm, having a well-established and respected base on which to build and capitalise.

Over the next four years a considerable sum of money was spent on enlarging the works and purchasing additional machinery, enabling production to be increased again. By this time, petrol lorries were becoming more readily accepted, but they were still not considered 'man enough' for anything other than light haulage, with all heavy-haulage work left to steam. And Fodens was undoubtedly the leading builder of steam wagons, claiming, in 1912, that it had sold over 1,000 wagons in 10 years. It was even achieving export sales, with a small but steady market in France and some sales as far away as Canada.

From about 1911 the 5-ton wagon was further improved by the introduction of smaller wheels, better brakes and springs, a slightly enlarged body, an enhanced driving position and detail changes to the engine. These were extremely well received and the works continued to be busy. All this activity at Elworth must have been the envy of others, for many manufacturers were struggling to keep their heads above water. The continued growth in the steam-wagon market, aided in part by the steady improvement in road surfaces, saw a gradual rundown of road locomotive production, with the last one being built before the decade was out.

Strangely, even after the outstanding results of the 1901 trials, the War Office showed a lack of enthusiasm for the use of mechanised transport, and it was not until 1913 that it placed an order with Fodens for new wagons. The outbreak of World War 1 in August 1914, therefore, gave the War Office a problem, as the Army was still heavily reliant on horse power, possessing only about 200 self-propelled vehicles. Fodens' London agents, Scammell & Nephew (later to make their own mark as heavy-vehicle manufacturers), were instructed to requisition wagons and prepare them for military use. Around 100 were provided in this way within one month, and all were Fodens.

Steam wagons could not be used anywhere near the front line in the war zone, as the smoke from their chimneys and the glow from their

It is known that Fodens built steam road locomotives for showmen, but what is not such common knowledge is its manufacture of self-contained steam powerplants for the same market. One of these trailer-mounted units is illustrated, with its chimney folded down into the travelling position. It was used to power a set of steam swingboats.
John Sanderson collection

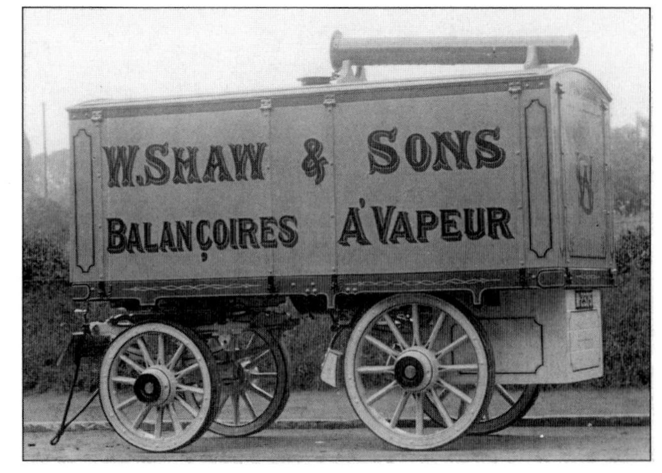

The 5-ton wagon was a modified and improved version of the earlier design, the changes having been made following the passing of the 1904 Heavy Motor Car Order. This allowed an increase in a vehicle's unladen weight to 5 tons and a legal speed limit, for a wagon without a trailer, of 12mph. The most obvious visible change is that the rear springs are now mounted inboard of the wheels, which are now of Fodens' characteristic Y-spoked design. It is possible that this steam bus may have been the works' first band bus, pre-dating the famous 'Puffing Billy'. If so, access to the high-mounted body could not have been easy when carrying brass band instruments.
Ian Allan Library

A working view of a 5-ton wagon and trailer, a combination that was allowed up to a maximum combined gross weight of 20 tons. The driver's seated position, with one leg outside the chassis frame, can clearly be seen. The trailer is a converted horse dray with the driver's lofty seat still in place.
Ian Allan Library

This 1913 6-ton wagon, works No 4086, was rescued from Australia for preservation in 1979. A 'Colonial' type wagon, its boiler had been modified to enable it to burn wood as there was no coal in the area in which it worked. When photographed on a damp day in October 1980 it formed part of the late Tom Varley's collection, other examples of which can be seen in the background. *Author*

GC 5832 is a 1928 'C' type tractor, chassis No 13196. It was new to Atlas Transport & Shipping of Chiswick, West London, and was then used by Messrs Camroux, London coal merchants, for coal haulage. Towards the end of its working life it drove a screening plant attached to its front end. It is now in preservation and was photographed in 1996. *Tony Peacock*

GC 5832
Foden

The 'C' type wagon was without doubt the definitive wagon of its type. The double-crank compound engine developed 25hp at 450rpm and drove the back axle through a three-speed transmission and Renolds chain. Under extreme operating conditions it was possible to operate both cylinders at high pressure, thereby increasing output by approximately 75%. Ackerman steering was now used, giving the driver much more accurate control.
This is a fine example of the six-wheel derivative, the 'K' type, able to carry 10-12 tons. The rear axle was connected to the intermediate axle by a roller chain. The steam-roller load completely fills the wagon's body space, and was presumably loaded by way of a loading dock.
John Sanderson collection

The 'C' type wagon represented the ultimate overtype design and was an extremely competent machine. TU 3113, production No 12388, dating from 1926, is a 6-ton, three-way tipper, new to W. J. King of Bishop's Lydeard, Somerset. Used for only five years, it was then left derelict until rescued for preservation in 1988.
Tony Peacock

firebox doors would have made them easily-recognisable targets for enemy gunners. They did, however, do invaluable work carrying materials for road building and maintenance, together with timber for the infamous trench system. The Army must have been impressed with the performance of its Fodens, as the factory was put under Government control and all the output was requisitioned, many hundreds being supplied whilst the war raged. The company also produced heavy-artillery shells during the conflict, putting tremendous pressure on production capacity. In fact the spare parts situation became so critical that the directors went against their principles and arranged for the manufacture of fireboxes, boilers and various smaller components to be sub-contracted.

The end of the war in 1918 brought problems of a different nature, with a large surplus of both steam and petrol vehicles, all being sold off at much less than their new equivalent cost. Fodens still managed to maintain steady sales but the directors were aware that outside pressures were mounting against the overtype wagon design. During the war the police had voiced their concerns over the poor visibility for drivers of this type of wagon, and had advised manufacturers that they expected to see improvements in this sphere, together with improved braking systems and more accurate steering than that provided by the traction engine type of chain-operated centre pivot. The potential problem was compounded when the postwar age brought an increase in road-traffic volumes with a correspondingly high rise in accident rates.

Conscious of the need to be seen to be doing something, Fodens put in hand work on a new wagon design. Whilst competitors, notably Sentinel, were doing well with the vertical-boilered undertype wagon (ie with the engine mounted below the chassis frame), Fodens decided to persevere with what it did best, namely the overtype. The reasons behind the success of its wagons were their simple, robust design, coupled with excellent build quality, ease of servicing and economy of operation. The designers felt that the new machine should capitalise on these features, whilst at the same time updating the arrangement to give appeal to a more discerning market. Experiments were made with a 'Scarab' oil burner in an effort to broaden appeal, and this was offered as an option in the autumn of 1920, but tempted few buyers.

Few can dispute that the new 6-ton machine, designated the 'C' type, represented the culmination of overtype steam-wagon development. Whilst retaining the basic layout of its forerunners, it featured a boiler working under higher pressure (220-240psi) and had a three-speed transmission. The driver now sat in a more elevated position within the cab and enjoyed the precision of an Ackerman steering system. Various sprocket options were available to meet the needs of individual operators and, with the right gearing, a speed of 25mph was attainable. The first chassis was completed in the autumn of 1921, production starting the following year.

Despite the higher cost of a steam wagon, in comparison with its petrol-engined equivalent, the new model was favourably received by Fodens' existing customers and sold well — possibly better than could have been expected in an economic climate where depression was beginning to take hold. A deferred payment system was introduced in an attempt to increase sales, whilst, in an effort to provide more model variation, a 12-ton six-wheel model, the 'K' type, was developed. A further variant was an articulated, or 'flexible', six-wheeler, of which very few were sold. A tipper chassis, with the body operated by hydraulic water pressure, became a further option. As another example

TU 3113
The Foden
TON STEAM WAGON
Foden

KX 3340 was built as a 'C' type wagon. It was converted to short-wheelbase tractor layout in 1933 by the well-known timber contractor Boughton's of Amersham, and was used on timber-winching work until the late 1940s.
Peter Durham

Preserved in tanker form is works No 13316, a 6-ton 'C' type wagon first registered in London in 1929.
Peter Durham

of Fodens' desire to look after its customers, a works driver was sent out both to deliver a new wagon and stay with the operator for a week to instruct its new driver on how to run and maintain it.

By 1924 the effects of the depression had really begun to bite, and at that year's company AGM it was confirmed that only a handful of orders awaited completion. One of these was for use on one of the Royal Estates, this being the second such order to be gained by Fodens, giving it the right to use the warrant of appointment as steam-wagon manufacturer to HM King George V.

Later in 1924 the company suffered a setback which shook it to the core. This was the announcement by William Foden that he intended to leave the company, and indeed the country, and emigrate to Australia to take up sheep farming. He was 55 and felt that he needed to break his connection with steam wagons. Edwin, his brother, remained as the sole family member on the board. The blow that William's departure dealt the factory, whose workforce was so dedicated to the Foden family, was considerable.

The company had reached the end of an era in more ways than one, for the overtype wagon was now under constant pressure, threatened in the short term by a different class of steamer, and in the long term by a new rival that was waiting in the wings and which was set to revolutionise commercial-vehicle design and performance.

UU 1283
HORRELL BROS
STOKE CANON
Nr EXETER
Tel.
STOKE
CANON
208
5
HORRELL'S
CIDER

6. Changing Times: 1925-34

The early 1920s had been very profitable years for Fodens, with the gross profit figure peaking at just short of £235,000 in 1920 — a vast sum of money for those times. However, difficult times were just around the corner, not just for Fodens but for the country as a whole, with a worsening economic situation and increasingly restrictive transport legislation. The emergence and acceptance of the compression-ignition — or diesel — engine, as a serious contender with steam for use in heavier goods vehicles, was to prove to be almost a disastrous challenge for the board, and it was to be many years before the company reached such lofty heights again. The journey was going to be rough, and, at times, stormy.

Despite the superb strength and magnificent performance that could be achieved with the overtype wagon, even its most loyal supporters had to concede that its long horizontal-boiler layout meant that it could suffer water-level problems in hilly terrain. More importantly, it impinged on load space. Neither of these factors affected Sentinel, Fodens' most serious steam-wagon competitor, which was achieving good results and (more importantly) sales with its range of vertical-boilered, undertype-engine 'waggons' (Sentinel always spelt this with a double 'g').

It became increasingly obvious — although perhaps unpalatable — to many at Elworth that Fodens would have to make changes to its design policy. Eventually the decision to design an undertype wagon was made, perhaps influenced by members of the new management which had been brought in following William Foden's departure for Australia.

That the task of successfully introducing a completely new design would not be easy must have been fully understood at the time. Due to the economic depression, sales of new wagons were in decline. Fodens would also have to persuade its loyal overtype customers that the new undertype was superior, although for years it had proclaimed that the overtype was the better design. At the same time it would have to try and gain new orders from established (and, presumably, satisfied) Sentinel users. Finally, Fodens' own workers were also thoroughly entrenched in — and loyal to — the overtype layout, and would need convincing themselves. Interestingly, Fodens had patented a design for a shaft-drive undertype wagon in late 1923, so it can be seen that the germ of the idea had been in existence for some time, even if no positive action had been taken to bring it to fruition.

Almost as if to prove its continuing allegiance to the overtype design, the company produced a short-wheelbase tractor, intended for use with one or more trailers. This was the 'D' type, the first production model being delivered in June 1926. Whilst it proved to be successful in its own right, orders for overtypes were virtually non-existent and it was obvious that, if the company was to survive, drastic action would be needed. The real question was whether the decision to change had been left too late.

The prototype of the new wagon was first seen in 1927. Designated the 'E' type, it was offered to the market as either a four-wheel 6-tonner or a six-wheel 12-tonner. The vertical boiler allowed an increase in load space, but the cab layout was seen by many as a retrograde feature.The firebox door was on the nearside of the boiler, which meant that it could only be operated by a two-man crew, whereas an experienced 'steamhand' could both fire and drive an overtype on his own. A twin-cylinder engine was mounted across the chassis frame to the rear of the front axle, driving the worm-drive rear axle through a two-speed gearbox and shaft. A later version saw the boiler moved further forward in the frame.

The 'D' type tractor was a last-ditch stand for the overtype design. A powerful, short-wheelbase machine, it could easily cope with one or more trailers. Many were subsequently fitted with pneumatic tyres on the front wheels, whilst retaining the solid rubber tyres on the large rear wheels, as in this illustration. It was photographed in Lincolnshire in 1965. *Author*

The first steam wagon designed by any manufacturer to run on pneumatic tyres was the Foden 'O' type, announced in 1928 and built as a four-wheeler for 6 tons (the Speed 6), and in six-wheel form for 12 tons (the Speed 12). The pistol-design boiler effectively divided the cab into two, with the chimney venting through the rear of the cab roof. The boiler's working pressure was 275psi, providing very dry superheated steam to the twin-cylinder engine with 5in bore and 7in stroke. There were three cut-off options and a two-speed gearbox with direct drive in top. Illustrated are two early examples that are believed to have been show exhibits. *Ian Allan Library*

An unusual design feature of the 'O' type was the stayless inner firebox crown, with the coal chute welded to both the inner and outer boxes. The welds were particularly inaccessible and there were fears that the difficulty of welding them evenly could lead to uneven rates of expansion. Insurance companies were wary of this aspect, giving problems to potential users. This is a later Speed 6, with full-depth front panelling, painted and sign-written prior to delivery.
Ian Allan Library

The modern appearance of the 'O' type is exemplified by this Speed 12 tipper demonstrating its side-tipping ability. The windscreen was made to follow the curvature of the front panels by being divided into three sections, behind the central section of which can be seen the 'By Appointment' coat of arms. The water tank is mounted behind the cab in this example. *Ian Allan Library*

In its day the 'O' type steam-wagon range was a very radical and modern design, that could run at 40-50mph with ease and in complete silence. Only a breath of escaping steam condensate when running would proclaim that it was a steamer. But it was to be a lost cause and it was to the diesel engine that the transport world turned. Only just over 130 Speed 6 and Speed 12 wagons were built so it is remarkable that any have survived at all. Chassis No 13750, a four-wheel Speed 6 dating from 1930, ran commercially for King's of Bishop's Lydeard, in Somerset, but was taken out of service before World War 2 and left to rot. It is now in the course of restoration and is seen here in a partially-restored state.
Courtesy Richard Parkinson

VM 4536 is a 1928 'C' type wagon, works No 13120. Now preserved, it was delivered new to Openshaw Brewery, Manchester, remaining in ownership until 1934 when it passed to Joseph Ashworth & Sons, cattle-feed merchants of Frodsham, Cheshire. At some stage in its life it was returned to the works to have new wheels and pneumatic tyres fitted. Its working life ended in 1957 after a spell with Scientific Roads Ltd, of Queensferry, North Wales.
Eric Sawford

The 'E' type was a heavier vehicle than the 'C' type and had a reputation for being expensive to run. Whether this made any difference to sales it is difficult to say, but just over 50 were sold. This was actually quite a creditable figure as, during its production run, the depression worsened and matters were not helped by the 1926 General Strike. It has been said that this may have had the effect of turning public opinion against the miners in particular, and against coal in general, giving rise to the theory that anything that was coal-powered was old-fashioned. The works continued production for the duration of the strike, although whether out of loyalty to Fodens or out of a fear of job losses is not known.

Sales of the 'E' type were definitely more difficult to achieve, and it is now open to debate as to whether there was actually 100% commitment to the undertype at Elworth. Certainly the wording of some of the company's advertisements at the time still appeared to be biased towards the overtype. In an endeavour to gain sales of any kind the company produced a small number of tractors, mainly for export, together with some railway locomotives using 'E' type components.

Competition from petrol-engined vehicles became more intense and the traditional types of steam wagon now looked very dated by comparison with the newcomers. A further factor that worked against steamers was the 1928 Finance Act, which allowed a 20% rebate on road tax for all heavy motor cars fitted with pneumatic tyres, thus effectively killing off solid-tyred vehicles, which included all steam wagons.

VM 4536
12
CHESTER
235
JOSEPH
ASHWORTH
& SONS
CATTLE FOODS
Frodsham
Bridge
Foden

Even though the diesel engine soon proved its mettle, there were those at Elworth in the early 1930s who doubted its ability to cope with heavy loads. Here, a trial has been arranged using a diesel lorry chassis to haul three dead steam wagons: two 'C' types and a Speed 6 — the latter with weights visible on its body.
John Sanderson collection

First exhibited at the Public Works Exhibition in London in November 1931 was the short-wheelbase 'O' type tractor for the haulage of loads up to 12 tons. The vehicle seen here, lettered in the ownership of Warwickshire County Council, has the cab set further back than on the wagons and is fitted with a neat chariot-style body. The heavy spare wheel cannot have been easy to deal with from such a high mounting.
John Sanderson collection

Whilst the 'E' type had suffered from its fair share of problems it had, nonetheless, started to win followers. Perhaps with this in mind, the management set the wheels in motion to produce the ultimate steam wagon; labelled the 'O' type, it was to be built in both four- and six-wheel versions, to be known as the 'Speed 6' and 'Speed 12' respectively. They were announced in 1928, being exhibited at the 1929 Commercial Motor Show, and were the first steam wagons to be designed from the outset to be fitted with pneumatic tyres.

The 'O' type featured a pistol-type boiler which provided very dry steam at 275psi to a twin-cylinder engine, driving by shaft to the 40 x 8 pneumatic tyres, and could easily run at more than double the then-current 20mph legal maximum for such a vehicle. In fact it could run at 45mph, provided it didn't run out of steam, this being a design fault with early machines that required modifications to the boiler and firebox. Just over 130 were built before production ceased in 1932.

Whilst all this work on the perfection of the steam wagon was proceeding, no-one could really have failed to notice the advances in design technology being made to the compression-ignition engine, which was being developed by several manufacturers with varying degrees of success. The board at Elworth now only had one Foden family member on it — Edwin Richard, who was eager to try the new engine. Unfortunately, he found himself overruled by the majority of the other directors who still maintained a strong loyalty to steam. Reports of dissension at boardroom level were rife and must have been felt further down the company structure, not helping the overall situation; neither did the appointment of 'non-transport' men to positions of power within the company, a succession of general managers being appointed in the hope of solving the company's problems.

A last attempt to keep steam vehicles in production was mounted with the 'Sun' tractor. This utilised the same boiler and engine as the Speed-series wagons, but the engine was mounted on top of the boiler. The motion-work was fully enclosed and drive was by chain to the rear axle. The water tank was mounted transversely at the rear of the cab, beneath the driver's seat and coal bunker. It was, however, doomed from the start, as by the early 1930s numerous kerosene- and petrol-engined light tractors were on the market which were cheaper to buy and took less time to start from cold at the beginning of a day's work. *John Sanderson collection*

Finally, in 1930, a decision was made to let Edwin and a small team explore the possibility of using either a petrol or diesel engine as an alternative power source, and in the autumn of 1931 Fodens' first diesel-engined lorry was completed. Powered by a Gardner 5L2 engine, it drove through a Daimler gearbox. It proved itself in tests, and was later sold to a Cheshire operator for whom it gave many years' service. Trials were run with other engines, both petrol and diesel, but none was satisfactory. Meanwhile, the majority of the management still showed a remarkable reluctance to say farewell to steam, and a small number of specialist orders continued to be fulfilled. Indeed, further effort was put into continuing steam-wagon development with the 'N' and 'Q' types, and, although neither really progressed beyond the prototype stage, much time, money and effort was expended on them that could have been better directed elsewhere.

It was to be an external influence that would prove the death-knell of the working steam wagon, other than for specialist purposes such as tar-spraying. This came in 1932 in the Salter Report for the Government. Amongst its recommendations were a maximum laden axle loading of 8 tons, and a sliding taxation scale on commercial vehicles based on weight, with advantages for any vehicle fitted with pneumatic tyres. These proposals were incorporated into the 1933 Budget, becoming law from 1 January 1934. Steam wagons, by virtue of their necessarily heavy build, were at an immediate disadvantage, weighing nearly 2 tons more than an equivalent petrol or diesel wagon, with the further handicap of having to carry a ton of water and fuel. They instantly lost favour, many being withdrawn from service with almost indecent haste, even though their fuel wasn't taxed.

Now, more than ever, there was a need for the diesel lorries that Fodens' management had shown so little interest in sanctioning, but total commitment towards the diesel still seemed to be lacking; the

This view of a chassis for one of the last steam wagons clearly illustrates the sloping-boiler layout which was built the opposite way round to a conventional steam engine. The underslung engine, propshaft and rear-mounted water tank are also clearly visible. *John Sanderson collection*

THOS FOX & SONS LTD
THOS FOX & SONS LTD
Market Place
BLACKBURN
PHONE
51613
Foden
Diesel

◀ AMA 105 (chassis No 15202) was Fodens' 101st diesel-engined lorry, an 'R' type that was built in 1933. Early in its life it suffered fire damage and received a streamlined 'Jubilee' cab and a new radiator. It is fitted with a Gardner 6LW engine. New to A. Giles of Toddington, it later ran from a Scunthorpe steelworks before passing to a Birmingham amusement caterer. Since preserved, it was photographed at a rally in 1978.
Author

◀◀ Chassis No 16266 was one of three new to J. J. Hadfield Ltd, bleachers and dyers of Chinley, near Whaley Bridge, in 1934. During World War 2 it was sold to an owner in Chapel-en-le-Frith and was fitted with a cattle-truck body. Taken out of service in 1947 it was then abandoned in a field. Subsequently saved for preservation, it still retains its original Gardner 4LW engine. It was photographed at Harrogate in 1999, painted in the colours of its new owner.
Author

Another product of the early-1930s transitional period was this neat articulated lorry. It appears to have been very close-coupled, with little room between the back of the cab and the front headboard of the trailer.
Ian Allan Library

This works diesel lorry is seen whilst on a road test in early 1933, parked near Buxton. The front wheels are of the same type that were fitted to some of the last steam wagons, as parts were being used up from existing stocks.
Ian Allan Library

company continued to produce steamers, together with a motley assortment of petrol and diesel vehicles, many of which were unreliable. For 1932 a trading loss of £48,000 was recorded. The situation became untenable for Edwin and he resigned, leaving no member of the Foden family on the board.

It is really outside the scope of this book, but Edwin shortly afterwards set up in business just down the road from the Elworth works and, together with his son Dennis and the designer Ernest Sherratt, founded E. R. Foden & Son, later to become better-known as ERF.

These were difficult times for all manufacturers, with many companies failing, and it is to Fodens' credit that, notwithstanding its internal problems, it soldiered on.

Perversely, the famous works band was going from strength to strength, winning the National Championship regularly and replacing its famous 'Puffing Billy' steam coach in 1933 with Fodens' first diesel-engined bus chassis, named 'Bandmaster'. This small venture into bus production must have provided good publicity. Ten PSV chassis were manufactured at this time, although only five were sold. Three were kept by the company, one was used as a tanker and one other as a horsebox.

A single-deck bus and a coach were on the company stand at the 1933 Olympia Show, together with a 30cwt petrol-engined lorry and a 4-ton diesel lorry powered by a Dorman-Ricardo engine. This was the first show at which no steamers were present.

At this stage the company appeared to have lost its way, whilst most of its rivals, including the fledgling ERF, had taken their first steps in the right direction. The concern was whether Fodens had left it too late and was at risk of disappearing from the scene altogether.

AMA 271 was the first Foden bus (chassis No 15284), built in 1933. It was basically an 'R4' type chassis, fitted out with a 26-seat coach body and powered by a Gardner 5LW engine. Used by the works band, it was named 'Bandmaster', and remained in service until after World War 2. *Ian Allan Library*

A standard 10-ton, six-wheel, 'R' type wagon, powered by a Gardner 5LW engine and equipped with large-section balloon tyres on the rear bogie. *Ian Allan Library*

The early 1930s were years of uncertainty for Fodens, fighting a rearguard action with its last steamers, and unsure of the way forward. Considering it had always been involved in heavier vehicles, the decision to market a 30cwt petrol lorry as part of its new product range now appears to have been a strange choice. Engines were supplied by Austin or Meadows, but the design was not a success. *Ian Allan Library*

7. Dieselisation and Rationalisation: 1935-8

Even to those with only basic business awareness it must have been apparent that Fodens was in a very precarious state, with the market for its 'bread and butter' machine, the steam wagon, killed off, and no clear plans for a replacement.

It will be recalled that in 1924 William Foden had left to take up sheep farming in Australia, and there were now those at the works who saw him as the only saviour for the company, even though his stated intention was never to return to manufacturing. Eventually, in desperation, a group of staff sent a communication to him which, by happy coincidence, arrived at a time when he had already planned to return to England on holiday, and he agreed to visit Elworth to see the situation at first hand.

What William saw when he arrived shocked and dismayed him — a company in disarray with no positive plan of action, and staff morale decimated. To him it must have been far worse than for anyone else; his family name had been brought down — the very company that he and his father had built up had been brought to its knees with a poor product range, unreliable products and a loss of faith with its all-important customers. An examination of the books showed exceptionally-large stock figures, much of it dead stock, and poor financial controls in many areas, with some jobs being completed at a loss. Drastic action was obviously needed to save the company from an untimely demise.

Just what thoughts passed through William's mind we shall never know, but he agreed to accept the Chairman's request to return, even though he must have felt like walking away from the disastrous situation that he had discovered. Naturally, he had to wind up his affairs in Australia, and it was not until 1935 that he found himself in a position to tackle Fodens' problems. On his return he was immediately co-opted to the board and, in August 1935, he accepted the post of Managing Director.

▶ Apparently a normal 4-ton dropside lorry, but unusual in that it is powered by a Gardner three-cylinder engine. This vehicle, new when photographed, had clearly been sign-written to a high standard.
Ian Allan Library

▶▶ Now in active preservation, RV 4328 is a 1933 model that was bought new by Portsmouth & Brighton United Breweries Ltd. After working for two more owners it then lay derelict for 12 years before being rescued for preservation.
Peter Durham

AJB
AJB
A & J BULL
CHELSEA MITCHAM
KEN. 5867
Foden
Diesel
GARDNER
RV 4328

A standard 15½-ton eight-wheeler, powered by a 6LW engine, sports the 'Jubilee' streamlined cab, introduced in the Jubilee year of 1935. Whilst being very stylish, the cab was not without its problems, creating blindspots for the driver who was so far away from the windscreen that it was virtually impossible to wipe clean when it misted up. The backward rake of the screen also caused problems in winter, in that it tended to gather snow which would not fall off and gradually built up, restricting the driver's vision. Whilst looking every inch a heavyweight, this vehicle impressively weighed less than 7 tons unladen.
Ian Allan Library

William, or 'Mr Willy', as he was known, must have had a clear, incisive mind, capable of dealing with a wide variety of problems simultaneously, for everything involved with the day-to-day running of the company required investigation followed by total reorganisation. At the same time a clear-cut decision had to be made on a range of vehicle models, followed by the design details.

The range on offer had developed in a haphazard fashion and it was clear to him that a policy of rationalisation on a range of diesel-engined vehicles was long overdue. A series of four-, six- and eight-wheel chassis was proposed, with a 4-ton lower limit, various attempts at lighter models not having been successful. All were to be powered by one of Gardner's current series of engines, with the chassis having as much component interchangeability as possible, cutting down on spares stocks and also making matters easier for operators.

Steam vehicle production was finally wound down at about this time when the last 'D' type tractors were built. In 1935, the 'O' type demonstrator was sold for evaluation purposes to Henschel in Germany, where the Nazi-controlled Government had authorised experiments with steam wagons in a bid to find suitable alternatively fuelled vehicles, reducing the country's reliance on imported fuel oil.

Once the company had settled on a policy and design strategy, the question of new vehicle orders then became paramount, as the haulage industry's faith and confidence in the Foden marque had been severely dented, and towards the end of 1935 there were very few outstanding orders. A sales team, headed by William himself, was formed with the task of transforming this unsatisfactory situation.

Out of sheer necessity the company bravely exhibited at the Olympia Show in November 1935, managing to win orders for 30 vehicles. Whether this was attributable to the new range, the 'salesmanship' of the team, or the fact that many prospective purchasers felt reassured that a member of the Foden family held the reins again, will never be known; most likely it was a combination of all these factors.

This striking lorry, seen on test in 1934 or 1935, utilised some cab styling from an SDG6 coach that was built for Whieldon's in 1934, giving it a design that was years ahead of its time. It would appear that it never got beyond the prototype stage.
Ian Allan Library

BMB 634 (chassis No 16404) was a 1935 TG5 chain-drive timber tractor. One of two prototypes, it featured a Gardner 5LW engine mounted transversely behind the cab, which placed its weight over the driven axle. The front axle was transversely sprung and above and slightly behind it can be seen the winch, whilst an impressive land anchor is placed centrally between the two axles. During World War 2 it was rebuilt to a conventional STG5 arrangement.
John Sanderson collection

Squat and powerful are the immediate impressions gained when looking at this 1936 12-ton tipper fitted with a 5LW engine. One of the hydraulic tipping rams can be seen in front of the intermediate axle and 'greedy boards' have been fitted to the body sides, extending them above the line of the cab roof which they had originally followed.
Ian Allan Library

Advertised as 'The hallmark of standardisation', the new designs were christened the 'Jubilee' range, having been conceived and planned in the Jubilee year of 1935. At the top of the range was the heavyweight eight-wheeler, designed for a 15½-ton payload and with an unladen weight of under 7 tons. Below this there were some six- and four-wheel chassis that could be powered by Gardner's 6LW or 5LW engines, and at the bottom was the little 4-ton four-wheeler. This had an unladen weight below 50cwt and was powered by Gardner's economical 4LK engine.

Streamlining was very much in vogue in the mid-1930s, and Fodens was up to the minute in this respect with its 'S' type cab, featuring a windscreen that was sharply raked back and described by Commercial Motor as 'most pleasing'. Sadly, as with so many radical designs, it was not without problems and required later modification.

Samuel Jacksons took delivery of the first diesel Foden lorry in 1931, and was so satisfied with its performance that it took delivery of this well-turned-out 7½-ton model with dropside body early in 1938.
Ian Allan Library

A neat little 4-ton lorry for a well-known Yorkshire operator was completed in early 1938. Fitted with a Gardner 4LK engine, and with an unladen weight below 2 tons 10cwt, it was able to run legally at 30mph.
Ian Allan Library

GR 6970 is a 1939 four-wheel DG showman's van, in immaculate condition, and was photographed at Nottingham Goose Fair on 29 September 1964. The windscreen on the prewar DG cab was split into two on the driver's side — an easy distinguishing feature. The inherent strength and reliability of Fodens has made them a popular choice with showmen for many years and this popularity is evidenced by the large number of more recent models in use on fairgrounds to this day.
Author

GR 6970
BELL'S

The massive losses of the previous few years were turned into a tiny profit for 1936, but there was still a long way to go to regain customer confidence and loyalty, although the company's thinking was now along the right lines. Standardisation on the Gardner engine range, which already had a reputation for reliability and economy, was undoubtedly a major factor in what was set to be a success story, whilst the rationalisation of components and parts interchangeability released much-needed capital, easing some of the problems relating to the everyday running of the business.

The model range was further developed to cover the lower-weight end of the spectrum. An ill-conceived venture into the 2-ton market had been far from successful, due to engine problems and poor reliability. The model that was now introduced was for a 6-ton payload, known as the OG4/6, and was to prove itself a worthwhile addition to the Foden family, remaining available, in updated versions, for many years.

The revised 'S' type, or 'DG' series, was introduced to the public at the 1937 Earl's Court Show in London, where it was one of the star attractions. Featuring the new S10 cab (or the S9 for lighter versions), with its distinctive, curved radiator and cab profile, and with many major improvements, it was immediately liked by potential customers. The fact that they had faith in the new range was evidenced by the rate at which orders were taken; in fact, works production couldn't keep pace with the demand, and delivery dates began to lengthen. As a result new tooling and plant needed to be installed and extra men recruited. The company could safely be said to be back on course under William's guidance, making Fodens, once again, a force to be reckoned with in the commercial-vehicle marketplace.

This 1937 7½-ton tipper with a 4LW engine and steel body has the 'S' type cab that was a revision of the more extreme streamlined version. Nowadays, tyre servicing and replacement are the province of specialist companies, but in prewar days the driver would be expected to change a wheel if the need arose. On this machine the spare wheel sits neatly on the chassis frame between the two axles.
Ian Allan Library

As if to provide tangible evidence of the strength and durability of the marque, this elderly six-wheeler was considered to be worth updating by its owner, Shap Granite Co Ltd. Photographed outside the works of Bromilow & Edwards, it had been fitted with a new steel dumper-type body and hydraulic tipping gear. It is interesting to speculate on how many more years' service it gave in this form.
John Sanderson collection

A 1937-registered DG6/15, photographed in 1941 in wartime guise, with partially-painted-over sidelights, headlamp mask and white-painted mudguards.
Ian Allan Library

▼ At one time the British steel industry was of tremendous importance, and in Yorkshire the entire eastern side of Sheffield was covered by steel works manufacturing a wide range of products, including large castings which required heavy transport to move them. To provide this transport, the English Steel Corporation bought some Foden tractors. This GHT6/50, fitted with an eight-speed gearbox and double-reduction axle, was bought in 1938. In this posed view, taken prior to delivery, it is coupled to a 50-ton, solid-tyred trailer loaded with test weights. *John Sanderson collection*

▲ CGB 281 was a 1938 6-tonner, built for Cowan & Co — a well-known Scottish operator which was a cartage agent in the North East of England for the railway companies. This smart vehicle, with twin spot lamps and chromed bumper-bar and horn, was an exhibit at the Scottish Motor Show, Kelvin Hall, Glasgow in November 1938. *Ian Allan Library*

◀ The classic rigid eight-wheeler is epitomised by this 1938 DG6/15, built for a well-known brick manufacturer. Mounted on 38 x 8 tyres and with a 20ft body, it was powered by a Gardner 6LW engine. *Ian Allan Library*

This DG6/15 standard eight-wheeler, fitted with a 6LW engine, was photographed during the war complete with its load of an enormous tank. The driver is dressed in the typical 'uniform' of a heavy-vehicle driver of the time, and now provides us with a nice period touch to the overall picture. *Ian Allan Library*

The twin-steer six-wheeler, or 'Chinese Six', as it was more commonly known, had a period of popularity shortly before the war as a chassis for intermediate weight limits. This one is a 10-tonner, classified DFA5/10, fitted with the classic S10 cab. *Ian Allan Library*

CNU 294 is a late-1935/early-1936 OG4/6, fitted with the 3.8-litre lightweight Gardner 4LK engine, which produced 53bhp. This was a 6-ton lorry but a lighter version was produced for a 4-ton payload. This vehicle was supplied new to a manufacturer of preserves in Derby. Sold in the late 1950s, it became a farm lorry, subsequently being bought for preservation. *Author*

8. World Conflict: 1939-45

The late 1930s saw the Elworth works become a hive of activity, full production being the order of the day, together with an air of excitement and satisfaction in the locality, as the whole community directly benefited from Fodens' return to full employment and profitability.

Although even the most optimistic must have sensed that war with Germany was inevitable, there was too much happening at the Cheshire factory to allow time to be given to personalities and events in faraway Europe. The DG range was selling well, and resources had been found to manufacture the first prototype dumpers and a heavy-haulage tractor. Also on the production line were a series of chassis for the Army; based on the DG , and mainly of six-wheel configuration, they were to be fitted with GS (General Service) bodies. No fewer than 1,750 would be built during the course of the forthcoming conflict. Another part of the works was busy with outwork for Rolls-Royce, itself fully occupied with the manufacture of its famous range of engines for combat aircraft.

Although there was considerable pressure to meet deadlines it caused no problems, none of the work being difficult and most of it in line with Fodens' normal production routines. However, matters would soon become more exciting and complicated.

Modern weapons would be needed to win a modern war and, shortly after the outbreak, Fodens was approached to see if it could help develop and (later) build a range of cruiserweight tanks. The first model to be built was named the 'Crusader', and was to be assembled, in separate sections, by a group of individual companies. An obvious benefit of spreading production in this way — in different factories in separate locations — was that total loss of production would be avoided if one or more of the factories were to be bombed. Jigs for the hull, gun-mounts and transmission were all designed and built at Elworth, the engines being built by Ruston of Lincoln, under licence from Liberty in the USA, with small parts being sourced by the Nuffield group. It was a team effort, requiring a high degree of inter-factory co-operation and the maintenance of excellent transport links between all the sites. Amazingly it worked, with the first tank being delivered to the War Office in October 1940. A further design development was produced in the form of the 'Centaur', and, altogether, nearly 800 tanks were built during the war years.

During World War 2 Fodens built some timber-tractors for the Forestry Commission. These were to prove particularly durable, although by 1964 this one had reached the end of its working days. The sacking covering the broken driver's cab window and 'No water' scrawled on the front panel says it all! It was seen at Chipping Norton, Oxfordshire, on 1 August 1964, and it would now be considered a worthy preservation candidate, together with all the other vehicles in this scene. *Author*

Registered in 1941 in the Bristol area, this STG5 timber tractor must have put in a considerable amount of work before being restored. It now leads a gentler life on the rally field. *Peter Durham*

During World War 2 Fodens produced 1,750 general-service army lorries, mainly of six-wheel configuration and based on the prewar DG design. This example was sold to a showman when its army days were over and it is seen at Wistaston in Cheshire in 1964. In this instance the GS bodywork has been replaced by a flat-platform body. The original 13.50 x 20in tyres have been replaced by a smaller size, which look out of place under the large flat-section front mudguards, and the hefty front radiator bar has been retained. *Author*

This is an example of a 1941 STG5 timber tractor. These were based on a prewar design, featuring a five-speed gearbox, double-reduction hubs and a powerful winch, and an extremely short wheelbase of just over 8ft. This restored vehicle, JRF 446, is seen at Fodens' works in 1999. *Author*

An interesting sideline to the tank development work came when Fodens was requested to design and build prototypes for a tracked towing vehicle and a gun-crew carrier. The designs were subsequently approved but production was passed to another company, for Fodens was fully occupied with its existing work and also the manufacture of aircraft cannon shells. This latter project was outside its normal range of activities, entailing the mass-production of relatively small items as opposed to the almost 'one-off' assembly of large commercial vehicles. A separate department was established, staffed almost entirely by women, production starting in 1941 and running until 1944, by which time approximately 7½ million shells had left Elworth.

Other specialist work included the fabrication of parts for the Mulberry harbour construction that was used in the D-Day landings, and some armoured bulldozers for use in clearing blocked roads in France following the Allied advance into Europe.

More in keeping with the normal line of business was the building of 50 timber tractors for the Forestry Commission. These short-wheelbase vehicles were based on the STG5 that had been introduced in 1936/7, and featured a heavy-duty winch and land anchor. Powered by either a Gardner 5LW or 6LW engine, these proved to be very capable machines, many surviving to give years more service after the war in what was undoubtedly a very hard working environment.

Suddenly, after so many years of turmoil and fighting, the war ended, and with it the need for Fodens' wartime products. The question now was: 'Where do we go from here ?'

9. Postwar Progression: 1946-56

The return to peace was, naturally, welcomed by everyone, and there was an overwhelming desire to commit the war years to memory and to move on to a brighter future, filled with new and exciting projects. For Fodens, however, and indeed for all commercial-vehicle manufacturers, there were more pressing problems that required attention, not the least of which was how to meet the insatiable demand from haulage operators for new vehicles. These were required to replace those that had been literally run into the ground during the war, working all hours on a minimum of spare parts and often on a 'make-do-and-mend' basis.

Production capacity to meet this demand was not a problem, as space had been freed within the factory following the cessation of war production, but a real headache was the supply of raw materials, particularly steel. The Government had decreed that priority must be given to the export of manufactured goods, as the country desperately needed foreign income, the result being that priority for the supply of raw materials, already in short supply, was given to those needed for this purpose.

A further worry was the election, in July 1945, of a Labour Government with a firm pledge to nationalise road transport. Fodens' concern here was that, in the past, it had always tended to cater for — and be patronised by — operators of smaller fleets, or owner-drivers; if these were to be absorbed into a nationwide organisation, then which vehicle manufacturers would be chosen to meet its vehicle orders? As it turned out, these fears were not without justification for, whilst Fodens was used by the new British Transport Commission, the latter's decision to turn to Bristol for the heavier fleet vehicles must have affected Fodens' potential sales to this market.

The company had looked to Gardner to supply all its diesel-engine needs from the late 1930s, and over the intervening years Fodens' production had steadily increased. A question mark now appeared over Gardner's ability to meet Fodens' increasing demand for engines. The basic problem was that Gardner was supplying engines to a wide range of manufacturers, all clamouring for its power units, and Fodens had to wait its turn along with other customers. The decision was thus taken to put further development into a venture that had been conceived — and had achieved a degree of success — during the war years. This was the company's own design of a two-stroke engine. The prototype single-cylinder unit had been completed in 1943 and had first run in 1944. Whilst originally intended for military and marine applications, the potential for its use in road vehicles must have been seen, particularly as it was possible to achieve an excellent power/weight ratio with such an engine.The prototype had presented the designers with many new challenges, as this was innovative work on two counts. Firstly, Fodens had never built its own engines and, secondly, the two-

The S18 cab was the postwar replacement for the prewar-designed S10 and was introduced in 1947/8. This handsome eight-wheeler was fitted with quite an early example, being registered in the spring of 1948.
Ian Allan Library

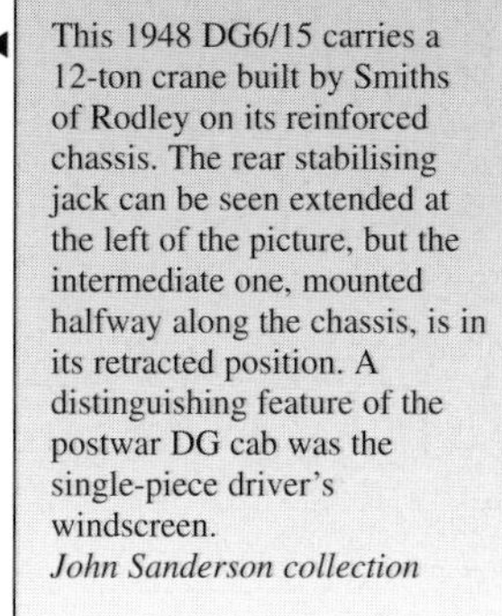

This 1948 DG6/15 carries a 12-ton crane built by Smiths of Rodley on its reinforced chassis. The rear stabilising jack can be seen extended at the left of the picture, but the intermediate one, mounted halfway along the chassis, is in its retracted position. A distinguishing feature of the postwar DG cab was the single-piece driver's windscreen.
John Sanderson collection

KBH 854 was a postwar STG5, new to W. G. Binder of High Wycombe in 1947, later passing through the hands of T. T. Boughton of Amersham. Chassis No 26276, it is fitted with a Gardner 5LW engine and a Foden six-speed gearbox. This view clearly shows the heavy-duty winch, with the guide rollers for the cable, and the impressive land-anchor. The spare wheel is fitted in its standard carrying position. It was photographed in West Yorkshire in November 1999. *Author*

stroke diesel design was a radical approach to the problem. Nonetheless, the company had a four-cylinder version running by the mid-1940s, although its public launch would not be until the 1948 Commercial Motor Show.

Whilst the experimental work was taking place it was, of course, essential to keep vehicles coming off the production line, in this case the prewar-designed DG models. To meet the demands of the postwar world, these had been modified, in particular by the fitting of an improved five-speed gearbox and servo-assisted brakes.

The Elworth works must have been an exciting environment in the late 1940s, for, in addition to all that has already been mentioned, plans were being made for a more aggressive entry into the bus and coach market — an area that had been tackled only very cautiously in the 1930s. Whilst being principally known as a lorry manufacturer, Fodens felt that here was a market in which it could succeed. Bus and coach operators, just like their road haulage counterparts, were in desperate need of new vehicles to replace those worn out after years of continual overloading during the war. There was also a general desire to shake off the influences of the drab recent past by the use of modern-looking vehicles that would be attractive to operators and riding public alike. The whole concept, which was to be the company's first new postwar design, was tackled with a fresh approach.

By the time that chassis No 24550, a six-wheel DG6, left the works in 1947, the DG did not have long to run, for it was shortly to be replaced by the FG series with the S18 cab. Although by that time somewhat dated, the DG range was widely regarded as a very handsome and reliable design, and one that had certainly been instrumental in helping to rebuild Fodens' tarnished image of the early 1930s. *Author*

Commercial vehicles are frequently altered and rebuilt in their working lives, unlike the average car, and often end up with an appearance quite different from that when they left the factory. HOR 659 is a prime example. Starting life in 1949 as a 5LW-powered haulage wagon with a five-speed gearbox, it was converted into the form seen here in the 1960s by Haslemere Motors, London. An export cab, Harvey Frost crane, 6LW engine and 12-speed gearbox have transformed it into this very capable-looking recovery vehicle, with looks that belie its true age. It was photographed at Fodens' works in Sandbach in October 1999. *Author*

The OG4/6 was to be the smallest vehicle in the postwar range. With an economical Gardner 4LK engine and a legal 30mph speed limit it soon became popular with operators, although availability was restricted by Gardner's inability to supply sufficient engines. The problem with Gardner was to lead to Fodens' decision to build its own, two-stroke engine. This particular vehicle for a South Wales operator dates from 1949. *Ian Allan Library*

The neat little OG4/6, built for a 6-ton payload and powered by a Gardner 4LK, sold readily from the late 1940s through to the mid-1950s, although a quality chassis such as this was to meet fierce and overwhelming competition from Bedford and Ford. Fodens wisely decided to leave this sector in favour of concentrating on the heavier end of the market, for which it catered so well. This 1948 model, new to Lloyds Packing of Manchester, is now preserved and was photographed at Harrogate in August 1999. *Author*

Until this time, most single- and double-decker buses were of the half-cab design, with almost square-section bonnets and exposed radiators, the only notable exceptions being those built by the 'Midland Red' company for its own use. Fodens' design was distinctively different. Although still of half-cab layout, it featured a stylish, full-width panel covering the radiator space, the bonnet line following the curvature of the top of the grille moulding. This was of a new and elegant design, later to be used on the goods-vehicle range. Neither was there a bulky nearside front mudguard, only a token moulding to contain wheel spray. A standard feature of the passenger chassis — designated the Series 4 or FP — was a cross-braced chassis mainframe, which performed well in tests, giving more rigidity and, therefore, greater strength, than a conventional design. The prototype, with a Willowbrook body, was completed in November 1945, and was used by Fodens as a demonstrator.

▼ The flat-fronted aspect of the earlier S18 cabs, with the flap that covered the radiator filler-cap, is well illustrated by this 1949 example. The bumper is of the style that is readily associated with the S18. Based in Northampton, it ran on contract to a firm of flour-millers. *Ian Allan Library*

◄ If there's a load to move there's a Foden to do it, and this example of a loaded eight-wheeler illustrates the point well. This FG-cabbed vehicle was supplied new in February 1950 to the impressively named Portsmouth, Gosport & Bognor Regis Gas Undertaking. It must have been new when photographed, as it would not have stayed in this condition for long on this type of work. *Ian Allan Library*

▲ After the war Fodens was quick to announce its first postwar design, the new PVD6 double-deck bus chassis. Despite its totally-enclosed engine area, it was claimed that maintenance was eased by the way in which the complete engine could be removed from the chassis. By removing the grille panel and radiator and disconnecting the controls, the complete engine and gearbox unit could be withdrawn forward on a trolley.

HMB 395 (chassis No 23000), with a Willowbrook 55-seat body, was built in November 1945. It was used as a demonstrator but later had its body removed, the chassis being sold to Warrington Corporation, where a replacement body was fitted and it was re-registered. *Ian Allan Library*

Warrington Corporation purchased several Foden buses for its municipal fleet.
OED 217 was the last PVD6 model built, chassis No 39832. Equipped with a Gardner 6LW engine and fitted with an East Lancs 58-seat body, it was delivered in March 1956 and was withdrawn from service on 30 September 1972.
Peter Durham

A separate sales department was established to deal with bus sales and, whilst modest successes were achieved with smaller operators, both private and municipal, it did not prove possible to break into the larger fleets that tended to remain loyal to the established bus-chassis builders for their postwar vehicle orders. Whether this was out of a conservatism which was not yet ready to accept Fodens' 'new look', or mistrust of a new player in the market, is open to conjecture. In fact, a little over 60 double-deck chassis were sold between 1948 and 1956, although single-deck bus and coach sales were to fare better.

In a drastic effort to make more impact on the coach market the company decided to produce what could only be described as a futuristic chassis design, with a rear-mounted engine. Whilst this was to become normal practice in later years it was radical for its time, and Fodens hoped to gain both useful publicity and sales in a market that was extremely buoyant. In the early postwar years petrol was still rationed and not many families owned a car, so that both day excursions and holiday trips by coach were commonplace, with operators vying with one another to have the smartest fleet. Coach designs, therefore, became of paramount importance.

The new chassis was exhibited at the 1950 Commercial Motor Show and at the 1951 Festival of Britain in London, which brought it to the attention of the general public. As a publicity measure this could not have been surpassed. This prestigious event was intended to show all that was new and best in Britain in all spheres of life, and tremendous crowds attended.

The chassis could utilise either Fodens' own two-stroke diesel engine or a Gardner unit and coachbuilders were soon attracted to the possibilities offered by the rear-engined layout. With no need for a conventional radiator grille, nor the half-cab arrangement, the way was left open for them to experiment with and display their postwar ideas, and a whole range of body styles, some quite flamboyant, were produced by a wide range of bodybuilders.

Summers weren't always good years ago, as evidenced by this wet scene in Rugeley, Staffordshire, in August 1963. Standing in the rain, outside Whieldon's Green Bus depot, is TRF 601, a PVD6 with Salmesbury body, seating 53. Dating from 1950 it was based on chassis No 29146. Whieldon's was a long-established Fodens customer, having bought one of the first buses produced by the company in 1933/4. *Author*

Foden coach chassis were often bodied by some of the smaller coachbuilding firms. ORB 952 (chassis No 30612), a PVFE6, was bodied by Bellhouse Hartwell. The styling seems to combine both streamlining and heaviness, a particularly unusual feature being the oval window set in the offside emergency-exit door. Delivered to Swain of Somercotes, near Alfreton, Derbyshire, in July 1950, it is seen parked by the River Trent on the Victoria Embankment, Nottingham, in May 1963, in company with some more period transport. Withdrawn in May 1965, it passed to Stewart & Cundy (breakers), also of Somercotes. *Author*

EWH 195, a PVSC6 with Whitson 35-seat observation-coach body, was built in June 1951 and supplied to Hargreaves of Bolton, which ran it until 1956. In 1958 it was bought back by Fodens to be used by the company's welfare department. At some stage in its life it acquired a Foden FD6 engine. It was photographed at a traction engine rally in Staffordshire in July 1963. *Author*

This PVD6, chassis No 27310, was used for some years as a demonstrator by bodybuilders Scottish Aviation, and was the only double-decker to be bodied by that firm. It was later sold to the Foy family of Glasgow, shortly before they acquired the business of Garelochhead Coach Services. It passed into preservation but, sadly, was later scrapped. *Peter Tulloch collection*

It had become apparent by the second half of the 1940s that the ageing DG-series lorry range would have to be replaced, as it was beginning to look dated, and the decision was taken to incorporate some of the front-end styling from the new bus range into a new cab design. The new series, designated FG, was introduced in the period 1947/8, sporting the handsome S18 cab, which was destined to last until 1956, the only modification in that time being the introduction of a slight vee to the front panels, replacing the flat aspect of the early cabs.

Development of the FE (Foden engine) two-stroke continued, and one particularly interesting aspect of it was that it was the very antithesis of Fodens' traditional diesel unit, the Gardner, renowned for its slow-revving, slogging pulling power. In contrast, the two-stroke was very free-revving, and, although sensitive to timing, gave a quick throttle response. Many Gardner devotees found it hard to adjust to the different characteristics of the new engine, but a two-stroke, used to the best of its ability and with full use made of the gearbox, could produce impressive results, as well as the charismatic howl so beloved by enthusiasts of the genre. Although shorter in length than the Gardner, it produced a much higher power output.

It was obvious to the engineers at Fodens that transmission systems would require modification in order that the new engines could be used to their full potential, and a series of experiments was carried out with gearboxes. This resulted in the announcement of the famous 12-speed box in 1952.

The same year, a modernistic look was extended to the goods-vehicle range when the FE4/8 lorry was launched. This 8-tonner used the four-cylinder two-stroke engine and had a smoothly-contoured, forward-control cab that sported an unusual and distinctive, low-mounted, diamond-shaped radiator grille. This cab was later phased out, as the two-stroke engine began to be fitted to heavier-payload models using the standard S18 cab and its successors.

A typical Foden coach of the early postwar era, LAE 906 was a 1948 Plaxton-bodied PVSC5 (chassis No 27378), supplied new to Russett of Bristol. *Ian Allan Library*

NWB 900 was a 1951 PVFE6 with a 35-seat Plaxton coach body, supplied new to Fantom's of Sheffield. Note the semaphore trafficator and the FG lorry-cab-type front bumper.
Ian Allan Library

The worthy successor to the DG series was the FG, an eight-wheel example of which, with the flat-fronted cab, is seen here. Model designation FG6/15, this 1950 machine was last used commercially on brick haulage in the Midlands. Now restored, and towing a four-wheel draw-bar trailer, it looks every inch the typical heavy-haulage lorry of that era. It was photographed at Harrogate in August 1999. *Author*

This FG6/15, built in 1950 with the flat-fronted cab, was new to Eastwoods Cement, London. As with so many of its kind it passed into showland use before being bought for preservation. It has now acquired the later-style S18 cab and sports the typical bumper that was used with it. As with so much that Fodens produced, the proportions of the whole vehicle look exactly right. *Author*

Delivered new to T. B. Lock & Sons, seedsmen of Yeovil, Somerset, this 1949-registered FG was a 7½-ton model fitted with a Gardner 5LW engine. Before it was acquired for preservation it worked for some years in showland, in the ownership of Anderton & Rowland, the well-known West Country amusement caterer. *Peter Durham*

ROBERT PHILP & SONS
Road Haulage
&
Threshing Contractors
Victoria
Foden
KYC 157

Both Fodens and its employees were obviously enjoying the challenges of the new-look era of the early 1950s. Just how they managed to start up so many new projects and designs, in differing realms of operation, whilst at the same time producing enough sales to pay the wages bill and overheads, seems nothing short of a miracle now, but achieve it they did, and in style.

Further forays into new ventures came with the production of some heavy-duty chassis to carry mobile cranes, and also some dump trucks. Another fresh enterprise was the building of some aircraft refuelling tankers, that were soon to be seen wearing the colours and names of many of the major oil companies. Larger versions of these were subsequently developed in line with the growth in aircraft size. These diversions were to reap rewards in later years and, as always, the company and its staff continued to learn, which was a benefit in itself.

Due to the need to export, Fodens had not been idle in this direction, with sales successes recorded in South Africa and Australia, and a growing demand from various parts of Europe. In its main overseas markets, subsidiary companies were established, providing a further boost to the parent company.

The year 1956 was to be a significant one for Fodens, which celebrated its centenary in style with a ceremonial parade through Sandbach. At the Commercial Motor Show later that year the new S20 cab was exhibited as a worthy successor to the S18. With its generous windscreen area, curved cab-corner panels and deep vee mouldings framing the proud Foden badge, it seemed to be a fitting benchmark for the company's 100th year.

This brings to a close a chapter which had been an exciting, rewarding and, above all, a satisfying one in the company's proud history, leaving it at the forefront of commercial-vehicle design and production. Fodens' second century was looked forward to with an air of optimism.

This is a 1952 example of Fodens' PVRF6 coach chassis. The cross-bracing of the chassis frame can clearly be seen, as can the control linkages running rearwards to the engine and gearbox. It has been said that these long linkages to the constant-mesh gearbox, and the driving position so far away from the engine noise, gave some drivers gearchange problems. Conversely, there were those who experienced no problems and enjoyed the performance of this machine, the design of which was undoubtedly ahead of its time. *Ian Allan Library*

Fuller's of Netherfield, on the outskirts of Nottingham, owned this 1951 Whitson-bodied rear-engined coach (chassis No 31238). This view, with the engine cover raised, highlights a drawback of the design — the loss of the conventional rear boot space for passengers' luggage. The direction-indicator arrows provide a nice period touch. *Ian Allan Library*

Observation coaches enjoyed a brief spell of popularity in the 1950s and this PVRF6, dating from 1952, is a Whitson-bodied example. Despite its impressive appearance it only seated 39. Salopia of Whitchurch owned several Fodens and some of the fleet can be seen in the background. *Ian Allan Library*

NTU 125 was a 1951 PVRF6 with a 41-seat Metalcraft body, supplied to Hollinshead of Scholar Green, not far from Sandbach. The body was of a more restrained style than many that were built on the rear-engined chassis, particularly by some of the smaller coachbuilders.
This coach remained in service until 1971, by which time only a few Foden coaches were left operating in the UK.
Peter Tulloch collection

Fortunately for the enthusiast, every so often a company introduces a really innovative design which breaks away from all conventional thinking. Mann Egerton was one such company, producing this one-and-a-half-decker coach on a Foden chassis. Seating 50, it was exhibited at Earl's Court in 1952. As with so much that dares to be different it did not prove popular, and few were built. *Ian Allan Library*

Looking every inch a working lorry is this preserved FG6/15, dating from 1954 and seen at Fodens' works in 1999. New to Marley Tiles, and registered in Kent, it is believed to have worked for that firm in the Burton-upon-Trent area before passing to a showman in Derby. *Author*

It was in 1952 that Fodens announced its first two-stroke-engined lorry. The 8-ton FE4/8 featured an eye-catching cab, with a distinctive diamond-patterned grille. This preserved example was fitted with a 2.72-litre version of the engine which produced 84bhp at 2,000rpm. It carries a 1954 West Riding of Yorkshire registration, although it is known that at some stage in its life it ran in the Leicestershire area for Thos Burton of Market Harborough. It was photographed at Harrogate in August 1989. *Author*

TRANSPORT CONTRACTOR
F.&F. ROBINSON
(STOCKTON-ON-TEES) LTD
EST·1910
(STOCKTON-ON-TEES) LTD
NWU 795
K.DICKENS
NORTHWICH CHESHIRE
R.C. CRESSWELL

The Foden two-stroke 8-ton lorry, the FE4/8, was launched in 1952 and featured a smoothly-contoured, rounded three-man cab of modern appearance, although, perversely, it was fitted with rear-hinged cab doors of a style that were later outlawed as dangerous. An example is seen here on road test, loaded with concrete blocks for load simulation. *Ian Allan Library*

By the early 1950s Fodens was beginning to produce purpose-built dumpers such as this 12-ton FGD6. Powered by a Gardner 6LW engine, and with double drive (via a 12-speed gearbox and double-reduction gears) to the 15.00 x 20-tyred rear wheels, it certainly looked to be a very capable machine.
Ian Allan Library

Sam Longson Ltd was a long-established Fodens customer by the time this FG6/12 was delivered in 1954. It was fitted with a 22ft body and was shod with Michelin D20 tyres. This is the later-style S18 cab, with a vee-shaped profile and exposed radiator filler-cap. *Ian Allan Library*

This Nottingham-registered FG6/15 sugar-tanker was built in 1954. The tank body was of double-skinned, insulated construction on a hardwood frame. To load the tank it was first tipped to 45° and was then filled through the central filler-neck that can be seen behind and above the cab. The other neck was an air vent, to be opened whilst filling took place. Discharge was by gravity on early models, although this was superseded by blower discharge on later machines. *Ian Allan Library*

This mid-1950s FG5/7½ provided the basis for a lorry-mounted Rapier concrete-mixer, a market in which Fodens were to be used in quite large numbers in later years. *Ian Allan Library*

PBT 973 is a 1955 S18-cabbed, heavy-haulage tractor, type FGHT/50T. Constructed on a short wheelbase, and with a ballast-box-type body, it was built to the special order of L. V. Brooksbank of Hedon, near Hull, which used it until 1973, when it was bought for preservation. It was photographed at Harrogate in August 1999. *Author*

SGG 6 is probably one of the best-known Foden heavy-haulage tractors in existence. It was built in 1956, in six-wheel form — type FGHT8/80 — as chassis No 41502, and was fitted with an eight-cylinder Gardner engine. The cab utilised parts from the standard S18 and is somewhat dwarfed by the large radiator that was fitted in conjunction with the 8LW engine. The vehicle was delivered new to Gavin Wilkie of Glasgow, a subsidiary of Glasgow Hiring Co Ltd. That firm was subsequently taken over by Pickfords, for which SGG 6 ran, as fleetnumber M4371, until 1969. Taken into active preservation, it was converted to an eight-wheel layout in 1974. Now restored in Pickfords colours, it is regularly seen at rallies. *Author*

PICKFORDS
M4371
Foden
GARDNER
SGG 6
R.&G.A.MEE
SHIREBROOK
DERBYSHIRE
Tel: 0623 744225

By the mid-1950s Fodens was building dump trucks with purpose-built cab and bonnet assemblies; this one, believed to have been a demonstration model, sported a cycle-type mudguard on the front nearside wheel.
Ian Allan Library

This FRD6/45 grossed at 45 tons with a 28-ton payload, and was fitted with a 300bhp Rolls-Royce engine. An idea of its vast bulk can be gauged by comparison with the man at its side. *Ian Allan Library*

Pictured on the tarmac at an airport is a 1957 FETU6/24 tractor unit, coupled to a 6,000gal-capacity tanker for aviation spirit, built on a Carrimore drop-frame semi-trailer chassis. The tractor was powered by Fodens' own engine, an FD 4.09-litre, six-cylinder two-stroke diesel. When loaded the outfit would gross at over 30 tons. The whitewall tyres are a period touch, popular on cars at the time. *Ian Allan Library*

In the late 1940s Fodens started to become more active in export markets, and soon established a firm foothold in Australia. This FG6 tractor, coupled to a locally-built, articulated, single-deck bus body by Bolton, seated 52, and operated in the Perth area. It was one of a batch of four supplied to the West Australian Government Railways towards the end of 1948. *Ian Allan Library*

The Netherlands was for many years a major market for Fodens, and in 1952 the company established an operation near Arnhem, called 'Fodenway', to look after its customers. Less restrictive legislation in comparison to the UK meant higher gross weight limits and rigid 8s with draw-bar trailers were popular. Many, such as this example, seen in 1957, were fitted with locally-built cabs in preference to the standard factory-built cab of the time.
Ian Allan Library

This scene admirably captures the spirit of the archetypal British eight-wheel rigid lorry. The 1957-registered, S20-cabbed machine with sheeted load has gone forever, as have the bonded Liverpool warehouses, the cobbled roadway and the Austin A40 van. *Ian Allan Library*

An FE6/24 tanker built for Murgatroyd's Salt & Chemical Co Ltd, a local customer, in 1957. It was fitted with a six-cylinder two-stroke engine, a five-speed gearbox and double-drive rear bogie, and shod with 9.00 x 20 tyres. *Ian Allan Library*

The stylish S20 cab was introduced in Fodens' centenary year of 1956. This is an early example, dating from early 1957, and is seen in Chesterfield, Derbyshire, hauling two tanks of hydrochloric acid. *Ian Allan Library*

This mobile crane chassis/cab was built during the 1950s as type designation FC22. Powered by a Rolls-Royce C6FNL-210 engine, it would carry a Ruston Bucyrus 22RB crane, the lowered boom of which would fit snugly between the two cab units when in the travelling position. *John Sanderson collection*

10. New Designs for New Times: 1957-69

MHS 344 is a 6x4 heavy-haulage tractor, type FGTU8/80 (chassis No 42230), delivered new to McKelvie in late 1957. It was fitted with a Gardner 8LW engine, eight-speed gearbox and two-speed rear differentials. The crew cab is based on the standard S20. During the 1950s and '60s McKelvie & Co Ltd became Scotland's largest heavy-haulage business. The tractor ended its days on internal duties at Ravenscraig Steelworks. *Ian Allan Library*

Takeovers and the absorption of smaller commercial-vehicle manufacturers by larger conglomerates were now taking place on a regular basis, but Fodens succeeded in maintaining its independence. Times were not easy, however, due in part to the knock-on effect of the Suez crisis with its fuel rationing, and political unease meant that the home-market demand for lorries slumped, with sales of new units being particularly difficult to achieve.

Fodens decided — quite correctly, as events were to prove — that funding must be put into further design and development work. This had the short-term advantage of giving the company a high profile as new products were unveiled. In the longer term, it must have helped to generate sales, firstly by offering new and improved products and, secondly, by generating customer confidence in a company that was seen to be not standing still. This was becoming more important as, by this time, the somewhat staid image of the road-haulage industry in the UK was beginning to change. What we now know as 'corporate image' began to assume importance, and smart, modern vehicles helped to create that image. The world was speeding up, and those who didn't keep up with it — or, better still, keep ahead — got left behind, and Fodens was determined to be among the front-runners.

The 1960s were to see increases in gross weight limits, leading to a demand for more powerful engines that, at the same time, were more fuel-efficient. The driver's work was also eased, with the introduction of semi- and fully-automatic transmission systems, improved braking, and power assistance for both the clutch and steering. Better access for maintenance was another feature to which operators began to attach more importance.

Traditionally, cabs had been of composite construction, consisting of a timber frame clad with aluminium panels, but now Fodens decided to move into a different medium with the use of fibreglass for a new cab design. Developed in 1957, and designated the S21, it was marketed from 1958 and was available as an option to the traditional cab. Built to a striking design, featuring elaborate curves and bulbous wings, it was quickly dubbed the 'Sputnik', this being the era of Soviet space exploration and the name applied to the satellites. Introduced at about this time was the Mark III six-cylinder, two-stroke engine. Capable of producing 150bhp, this was something that was to make the opposition sit up and take notice.

Sadly, whilst the company had a range of excellent products, outside influences came into play, as political unrest and a series of damaging strikes in the engineering industry depressed the new-vehicle market. Wisely, Fodens decided to gain much-needed sales by way of specialisation, including marine engines, dump trucks, aircraft refuellers, heavy-haulage tractors, concrete-mixer chassis and bulk-refuse vehicles. The famous crane-carrier chassis also went into full production at the tail end of the 1950s. Once again, Fodens had proved that it was a manufacturer to keep an eye on, and was poised to take full advantage of better times when they returned.

Regrettably, the sale of bus and coach chassis had not achieved the anticipated results, although approximately 550 had been sold. There would appear to be no single reason for the lack of take-up but, sadly, the decision was taken to phase out production, although some specialised export chassis were built to individual order some years later.

A. Stevens & Co (Haulage) Ltd specialised in the transport of long-section steel from the Teesside steel works. The two-stroke-powered, S20-cabbed tractor dating from 1957 is here seen coupled to a very long, tandem-axle semi-trailer of Stevens' own build, fully loaded with cut steel plate. *Ian Allan Library*

COWANS SHELDON CARLISLE
McKELVIE & Co LTD
HEAVY HAULAGE SERVICES
McKELVIE & Co LTD
Mc KILVIE & Co LTD
MHS 344

509 ENK dates from 1958 and is fitted with the S20 cab. It delivered heavy-fuel oil for J. Cowell & Sons of Cheshunt, Herts and was acquired for preservation in 1990. It is seen here as it completed the Trans-Pennine Run in Harrogate, in August 1999. *Author*

The S20 cab is regarded by many as one of Fodens' most handsome designs and in this illustration is shown fitted to a 1958 FG5/14. This vehicle was new to Carmans Transport Ltd of Stoke-on-Trent as a chocolate tanker on contract to Nestlé. Subsequently sold to an owner in the Hereford area, it was used as a tar boiler, in which form it survived until 1988, after which it lay derelict until 1996 when it was saved for preservation. It was photographed at Fodens' works in October 1999. *Author*

Lorry sales were faring better. In 1959, purchase tax on commercial vehicles was withdrawn and hire-purchase restrictions eased, giving a boost to the transport industry. The first tentative steps towards building the UK's motorway network were taken, and with operators anxious to make full use of these new 'super highways', the manufacturers responded with more powerful engines and revised axle ratios.

By the early 1960s there was more confidence, both at home and abroad, where, in particular, the Middle East and Australia were proving to be worthwhile markets. To cope with the home-market recovery, a modernised production line was organised at Elworth and new tooling installed, enabling production to be maximised. At the 1960 Commercial Motor Show Fodens introduced its Mark IV engine, a turbocharged six-cylinder two-stroke of 4.09 litres, capable of producing 210bhp at 2,200rpm. This was probably the first commercial-vehicle engine to exceed a specific power output of over 50bhp per litre, and was fitted with an intercooler. It was exhibited on its own and also fitted to a FED6/30 dumper.

NESTLE'S
Foden
J.T. SANDERSON
Smallwood
Sandbach
FG 5/14 BUILT 1958
424 DMB

This interesting dumper, owned by Eastwoods Cement, is equipped with an S20 cab. It has been fitted with a heavy-duty bumper and grilles in front of the radiator and headlights as protection, and a sump-guard can be seen below the numberplate. The registration dates from early 1959. *Ian Allan Library*

By comparison with this picture we see here a heavy-duty, six-wheel, purpose-designed dumper, also dating from the late 1950s. This design became the standard formula and was very successful. Half-cabs are popular for dumpers, as they are less prone to accident damage and the driver's line of sight is improved. *Ian Allan Library*

Foden
21 G
MILLBURN

This KG6/20, with a 6LW engine, 12-speed gearbox and trailing rear axle, was new in 1961 to British Aluminium, Dolgarrog, North Wales. The colour scheme looks well on the elegant, bow-fronted S20 cab. Authentically restored, it was photographed at Harrogate in August 1999. *Author*

James Shipstone, of the Star Brewery, Basford, Nottingham, was a Fodens customer from steam days, and continued to be so until the Brewery was taken over and lost its individual identity. It was renowned for the high standard to which it maintained its fleet, and, reportedly, there was always a waiting-list of buyers wanting to acquire its vehicles when they were traded in. This 1962 lorry had been one of the fleet, and was photographed in West Yorkshire in June 1990. *Author*

The fibreglass S21 cab was offered as an option to the composite S20 from 1958 and its non-corrosive qualities have made it popular with showmen. This Surrey-registered, short-wheelbase tractor unit dates from 1959 and, as is so often the case, has been fitted with generators to provide power for the owner's ride and lights. It was photographed at the Lincolnshire Showground in August 1978. *Author*

In September 1962 the company created considerable interest at the Earl's Court show, where the star exhibit was an eight-wheeler chassis, model designation TE6/24. Equipped with a two-spring-suspension, lubrication-free bogie that was lighter than a conventional bogie, it also featured the first British-built tilt cab, giving excellent engine accessibility. This was the fibreglass S34, fitted with Cibie rectangular headlamps.

Through the early years of the decade plans were made for any expansion that might be necessary to take advantage of the demand for larger vehicles, operating at higher speeds, that was expected to result from revised legislation.

The workforce, the company and the local community received a sad blow with the death of William Foden on 2 June 1964. The man who had masterminded Fodens' recovery in 1933, who had been involved in almost every aspect of its growth and transformation into one of the world's most prestigious manufacturers, and who formed a last link with the company's illustrious steam past, was dead. A whole era had ended.

As if to give added weight to this statement, revised Construction & Use regulations arrived later in 1964 that were a body-blow to the rigid eight-wheeler, a chassis that for many years had been a constituent part of Fodens' product range and which had always enjoyed steady sales. The new regulations allowed articulated vehicles to operate up to a gross weight of 32 tons, whilst the rigid eight-wheeler was, effectively, limited to 24 tons. Fodens, and many of its customers, liked the inherent stability of the eight-wheeler and, in an attempt to make it a viable proposition again, the company developed a most unusual machine that was announced at the 1964 Commercial Motor Show. This was the 'Twinload', comprising an eight-wheel, rigid load-carrying tractive unit,

162 KPL
01-574 3237
DAWN OF THE CENT

The fibreglass S21 cab made a big impression on the transport world when it was announced in 1958. It made a bold statement, both for Fodens and for those operators who chose it as an option to the S20, which was still offered but was of composite construction. This superb flour tanker, 396 SFK, dates from 1962. *Ian Allan Library*

A nice publicity shot for both Ameys and Fodens. Ameys was using the S20-cabbed tractor in 1964 to haul a British entrant in the New York–Bermuda yacht race. The yacht, *Noryema III*, was owned by Mr R.W. Amey, Chairman of the Amey Group of companies. *Ian Allan Library*

coupled to a single-axle articulated semi-trailer, grossing at 32 tons. It was given the model designation 8AE7/32. Unfortunately, despite receiving acclaim at the show, the market was not ready for such an innovative design, and only a limited number were built. It was a sad end to a well-thought-out design.

Overseas markets continued to grow in importance, particularly for heavy tractor units and dumpers, whilst for the domestic market a succession of handsome new cabs were produced. Following the tilting S34 came the fixed S36 with twin headlamps, the S39 and S40, the latter being of steel construction and made by Motor Panels Ltd of Coventry.

Engine outputs continued to increase to meet the heavier demands being put on them; Fodens' Mark VII engine, introduced in the early 1960s, produced 225bhp, aided by exhaust turbocharging and an intercooler. This was more than double the output of Gardner's 6LW of barely 10 years earlier.

At the 1968 Commercial Motor Show the company once again produced a revelation in the shape of the metal S50 half-cab, with forward-sloping windscreen, primarily intended for construction-site work. Its sister was the full-front version, again with a forward-sloping windscreen and known as the S60, a fibreglass option being designated S70. It can be seen that Fodens strived continually to be innovative, but, as is so often the case, the radical new designs were cautiously received by a conservative market. Nevertheless, the 1960s ended on a confident note, and the next decade was anticipated as one of new opportunities.

MERICAN CHAMPION
Ameys of Oxford
TELEPHONE
OXFORD
35421
Ameys
NORYEMA III
CAMPER & NICHOLSONS LTD
SOUTHAMPTON, ENGLAND
VRX 110

Recreating a scene from the past is this preserved 1960 model KG4/14. When new it ran for James Shipstone's Star Brewery, Nottingham, for which it must have carried many barrels of beer.
Peter Durham

This handsome FG6/24, seen here with a well-sheeted load, dates from 1959 and was new to M. Elliott & Sons (Transport) Ltd of Bournemouth. Fitted with a Gardner engine, it was used on general haulage until 1970.
Peter Durham

M. ELLIOTT & SONS (TRANSPORT) LTD
M. ELLIOTT & SONS
(TRANSPORT) LTD
BOURNEMOUTH & WAREHAM
NORTHBOURNE 2812 BERE REGIS 205
Foden
19
GARDNER 150
THE EMPEROR
YRU 877

Shown here is a chassis/cab that has been built to Australian specification, with an additional, heavy-duty bumper, and cab-door wind-deflectors. Seen prior to despatch, it is shod with slave tyres. *Ian Allan Library*

The finishing touches are here being put to the 1962 Commercial Motor Show star exhibit. This eight-wheeler, type TE6/24, fitted with a Mark VI two-stroke engine, has the new S34 tilt cab. This was the first British tilt cab designed for quantity production and was counterbalanced by torsion bars, enabling it to be tipped forward with one hand. This was part of a policy of simplified chassis maintenance being pursued by Fodens, further moves in this direction including a two-spring, lubrication-free bogie — with the exception of the differentials, of course. Confounding those who said it could not be done without a weight penalty, it tipped the scales at a very creditable 6 tons 4cwt, giving a body-and-load allowance of 17 tons 16cwt. *Ian Allan Library*

Ready for delivery in 1963 to Ensign Tankers Ltd, part of the Slater Group, is this 24-ton-gross, S34-cabbed limestone tanker of 540cu ft capacity fitted with an air-discharge system. At the time that this photograph was taken the Ensign Tankers fleet was 100% Foden.
Ian Allan Library

TILT Foden CAB
Foden
FODEN 1962
Foden

The S21 cab survived well over the years due to its fibreglass construction, and a reasonable number can now be found in preservation. This example dates from 1961.
Peter Durham

The S34 tilt cab was introduced in 1962. This view shows the bodywork modifications made necessary, if a Luton-type body was fitted, to enable tilting to take place. The vehicle is being used to generate power, the cab being raised to allow more air to reach the engine. It has been levelled with blocks of wood placed under each of the nearside wheels. Photographed at Harewood, near Leeds, in August 1997, EUT 919C dates from 1965. *Author*

In recent years it has become more difficult to find crane-carriers in existence. This picture taken near Elgin in May 1999, shows a tired-looking UOA 125H, owned by B & L Cranes Ltd, of Burghead, south of the Moray Firth, Scotland. Fitted with a Priestman crane, it appears to have had a hard life.
Tony Peacock

The 'Twin-Load' concept was new to the UK when it was announced in 1964, but the idea was in use elsewhere in the world, particularly the USA where such vehicles were known as 'Dromedaries'. It was introduced as a result of a change in legislation which allowed articulated vehicles to operate up to 32 tons gross, whilst the rigid '8' was restricted to 24 tons. Grossing at 32 tons, each load platform could carry 11¼ tons, whilst the total vehicle length was 42ft 7in. Given the model designation 8AE7/32, it was unfortunately not embraced by the market and few were sold.
John Sanderson collection

The 'Low Line' crane-carrier chassis was introduced in eight-wheel form in 1963 and remained available until 1972. The cab was mounted ahead of the axles, with the engine and radiator slung low-down on the chassis frame between the front wheels. The roomy cab could accommodate a crew of four. A variety of engines was fitted, including Fodens' own FD6, Gardner's 6LW and 6LX and, from early 1967, the Leyland 680. For export models Deutz six- or eight-cylinder air-cooled diesels were standard.
John Sanderson collection

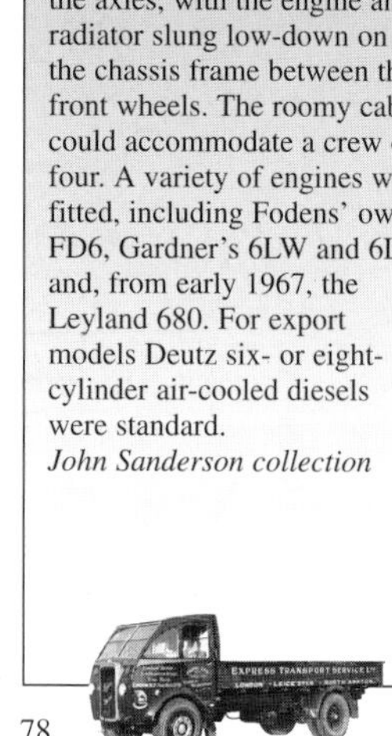

The crane-carrier chassis in 6x4 form was introduced in 1964. DLO 243C, dating from 1965, was owned by Wimpey Construction and carried a Ruston Bucyrus crane. It was seen working within the narrow confines of a City of London street in 1967. *Author*

The S50 half-cab was announced in 1968. Its principal application was intended to be on construction-site vehicles such as the concrete-mixer truck illustrated here. As these were only usually used on short-haul applications there was no need for a two-man cab, and driver visibility for difficult site access and manoeuvring was improved. A bonus for the operator was that accidental cab damage, particularly to the windscreen, was minimised. The theory behind the reverse-slope windscreen was that it would keep clearer in inclement weather than a conventional screen, at the slower speeds at which such a vehicle would normally be used. *John Sanderson collection*

▶ This two-stroke-engined FE4/16, LAU 323E, was another vehicle that was owned from new by James Shipstone. Dating from 1967 it later passed to Thomas Fox of Blackburn, and has now been in active preservation for a number of years.
Peter Durham

▶▶ CKX 374F was registered in Buckinghamshire in 1968. Powered by a Cummins engine, and sporting the S36 cab, it makes a handsome machine. *Peter Durham*

HEAVY HAULAGE
SIRE
EDWIN
JOHN MAYLE
Heavy Haulage
MANSFIELD
NOTTS.
1
CKX 374F

During the mid-1970s the standard articulated combination was a two-axle tractor unit coupled to a tandem-axle semi-trailer. This curtain-sided vehicle operating for United Glass is a typical machine of the period, although in this instance the trailer features a stepped layout. The cab on this S83 Foden could be tilted in about 80 seconds by the simple operation of an hydraulic cab-tilt pump, an improvement on earlier designs. It dates from 1975/6.
Ian Allan Library

11. Expansion: 1970-5

The start of the 1970s was full of optimism and confidence, born out of Fodens' long history of development, innovation, pride and stubbornness — the will to keep going when all the odds appeared to have been against the company; a company, moreover, that had a product range second to none, that had expanded into worldwide markets and, above all, that was respected and liked (some may even say loved) in the world of road haulage.

An event at the beginning of the decade more than amply demonstrated the company's financial strength and confidence. This was Fodens' bid to take over Atkinson Lorries Ltd, a relatively small manufacturer of premium lorries with a respected reputation. There was quite a degree of interest in this company, and a bid was also submitted by ERF, amongst others, but eventually the offer from Seddon was accepted by Atkinson's board. It is interesting to speculate where Fodens would be now if its bid had been successful.

Meanwhile, the works was busy supplying the needs of a buoyant home market for haulage vehicles, bolstered by crane chassis and dumpers together with the demands of a strengthening export market. By this time the model programme had been revised and production had been streamlined. At the 1970 show a six-wheel, twin-steer articulated tractor unit for loads of up to 38 tons was shown, together with an eight-wheel tipper for 30 tons, built in anticipation of revisions to Construction & Use regulations.

For the show in 1972 Fodens was the only manufacturer exhibiting a new cab — the boldly-styled S80. This could be tilted to 45° for maintenance access, the main driving compartment comprising a one-piece, box-like structure constructed of glass-reinforced plastic. Small panels that were vulnerable to damage in regular use were designed to be easily replaceable. With its angular lines set off by 11in headlamps it was an impressive styling exercise that caught media attention. Two new gearboxes were also on display: an eight-speed unit, and a torque-converter transmission developed with Brockhouse. With so much that was new the stand attracted considerable interest, and the future looked promising.

The only cloud on the horizon was a doubt that production capacity at Elworth would be able to cope with anticipated demand. Part of the problem was of Fodens' own making, in that the model range still utilised a high content of its own manufactured parts, whereas most other manufacturers bought in proprietary parts. This factor, coupled with the high percentage of output that comprised vehicles built to special order, as opposed to 'off-the-peg' models, meant that production was not as high as it could have been — and, indeed, needed to be, if Fodens was to continue to be a major player in the commercial-vehicle marketplace.

In a bold move the board of directors set aside the sum of £3.8 million to finance an expansion of the works. In fact, it was to be more than just an expansion, as the decision was taken to build a new assembly plant that would be one of the most modern of its type in the Western world. American assembly methods were looked at, but these were similar in principle to contemporary Fodens practice, so it was to Europe that the company turned with a view to studying existing plants. Various firms were studied, but it was the Scania-Vabis factory in Sweden that seemed to provide most of what Fodens wanted.

The objective was to build a new plant capable of producing a minimum of 80 chassis per week, with sufficient in-built flexibility to increase this if demand dictated. At the same time it was to be adaptable enough to produce anything from 'run-of-the-mill', four-wheel 20-tonners, up to massive dump trucks and, of course, the whole range in between. A computerised control system was to be an essential part of this ambitious project.

Fodens continually improved and updated its dumper-truck range, this model from the early 1970s utilising some of the pressings from the S50 cab.
John Sanderson collection

UNITED GLASS
UNITED GLASS
FODEN
U.G. CONTAINERS LTD.
CASTLEFORD
40 259
YORK
KWX 503P

One of the better-known haulage companies in the north of England is that of Robson's of Carlisle, famous for its named fleet. AHH 77K, 'Border Prince', fitted with an S39 cab, was delivered in 1972 as fleet No FD541. Here it is seen coupled to a low-loading trailer carrying an International crawler tractor. *Peter Durham*

The S39 cab had a two-piece windscreen which differentiated it from the S36. OEH 254K was new to Richardson's Transport of Stoke-on-Trent in 1971, being used for five years before being sold to a plant and machinery transport business. Taken out of use in 1988, it was bought for preservation in 1995. Now restored, it can usually be found coupled to a Boden semi-trailer. *Peter Durham*

Contractors started work at the end of 1972, and completed by August 1973. That such a large and complex system could have been finished in such a short time was nothing short of remarkable, but, even more importantly, it worked, and worked well, with production capacity rising to 80 vehicles a week. The key element was an overhead conveyor system, the 'main line' being the one on which the chassis were assembled, with ancillary parts being supplied to it by a number of separate, subsidiary conveyors. The company was now in a prime position to meet customer demand.

All that was needed was orders, and these came in as expected, as operators updated their fleets to meet the UK's revised regulations that had been introduced as anticipated. But the commercial-vehicle market is a notoriously fickle one, highly susceptible to outside influences and well known for moving in 'boom and bust' cycles. A series of strikes in the coal and energy-supply industries brought the three-day working week, and despondency took over from optimism, as sales of all commercial vehicles fell drastically. Price-cutting reared its ugly head, particularly amongst Fodens' foreign competitors — a situation that is always bad news as there are never any winners, only losers. How ironic, that the long-needed new assembly plant was now obliged to run at reduced capacity.

Nothing daunted, the company battled on, as it had had to do so many times in the past when faced with adversity. Fortunately, in the autumn of 1973, it gained orders for over 1,000 military vehicles from the Ministry of Defence. This was to provide work for two years and was estimated to be worth £10 million. It was an area from which there had been useful revenue for some years and which continues to this day. A new model was also developed; aimed principally at European

LEN BARLOW & SONS
HEAVY
HAULAGE
M 7
Laura
Thomas
2
GARDNER 180
OEH 254K

markets and named the 'Universal', it was announced at the Amsterdam show in 1974.

Sadly, the Universal's development costs, coupled with Fodens' system of building vehicles, brought financial problems. The root cause was the long supply-chain for raw materials for the manufacture of components, a high proportion of which were still being assembled at Elworth. A considerable amount of capital was tied up in these stocks — capital that would not have been taken out of circulation if ready-built components had been bought in from outside suppliers. This system also meant that a larger workforce had to be maintained, providing a further drain on capital which would have been better used to finance the day-to-day running of the company.

Financial assistance was obviously needed, but the company's bank refused help and, eventually, a Government-financed loan was negotiated out of a fund that had been set up to help companies with cashflow problems. Unfortunately, news of Fodens' cash difficulties soon became known — just the sort of publicity that every business seeks to avoid. None was more sensitive to this than the board of directors, who were, however, heartened by the favourable financial report on the company that had been compiled by the Government-appointed accountants. So cheered were they by this that they opted to approach the stock market for help, in preference to taking up the Government loan. This was achieved in the form of a share issue, whereupon funds flowed into the company, the Government's financial package wasn't required and Fodens fully retained its financial independence. Another battle had been fought and won, but would it be only a short-term gain ?

MSF 600P is a 6x4 S80 cabbed tractor, seen in West Yorkshire in April 1999.

By the mid-1970s Fodens was offering to fit more outside components including Fuller gearboxes and Rockwell axles, and this policy helped the company to remain competitive. This Gardner-powered eight-wheeler of the period is proof that, whilst articulated units were growing more and more popular, there was still a worthwhile market for the rigid eight-wheel chassis that continued to sell in reasonable numbers.
Ian Allan Library

12. The Storm Clouds Break: 1976-80

Whatever the financial problems behind the day-to-day running of the company, the design and development teams continued in their quest to improve its products, an early candidate being a revised version of the S80 cab, to be known as the S83. This was introduced at the 1975 Scottish show, and featured an improved tilt mechanism that allowed faster operation.

A surprise reintroduction in 1976 was of the old S39 cab on a new, six-wheel chassis, known as the 'Sixer', aimed primarily at the construction industry — in particular the truck-mixer market. Using many bought-in components, including brakes and axles, it weighed in at under 6 tons.

The real surprise of 1976, however, was the company's decision to re-enter the bus market with a rear-engined, double-deck chassis, designated NC. Developed in conjunction with Wigan-based coachbuilder Northern Counties, it was displayed at the Earl's Court show. Featuring an Allison automatic transmission system, it appeared to be favourably received by the bus industry, with Greater Manchester Transport agreeing to take two prototypes for evaluation.

◀ This 6x4, S81–cabbed, heavy-haulage tractor was new in July 1976 to Wimpey Construction, for use with a low-loader trailer for the haulage of heavy plant machinery. At some time in the 1980s it was returned to Fodens for uprating to 120 tons gross train weight, and at the same time was fitted with a 350bhp Cummins engine and a Fuller 13-speed gearbox. It subsequently passed to CKL Transport of Halifax before being bought for preservation. It was photographed in May 1998. *Author*

YYP 901T is another example of an S81 heavy-haulage tractor. This one was new in 1978 to Redhouse Industrial Services Ltd of Coventry, better known as Red House Motor Services (RHMS). It subsequently passed to Metcalfe's of Macclesfield, in whose livery it was photographed in 1997. *Author*

The S80/83 was a tall cab, and when fitted with a high body, as in this instance, it could look extremely impressive. William Percival's well-kept eight-wheeler, looking vast, was in Nottingham on 2 October 1994. *Author*

A surprise reintroduction in 1976 was of the old S39 fibreglass cab on a new chassis, known as the 'Sixer' and intended mainly for use in the construction industry. Usually powered by a Gardner 6LXB engine, it was an efficient vehicle of low weight and utilised a large number of outside components.
This one was photographed in August 1991. *Author*

Exhibited on the Northern Counties stand at the 1976 Commercial Motor Show was the Foden NC double-decker (chassis No 94050) in the livery of Greater Manchester Transport. The 75-seat vehicle was powered by a Gardner 6LXB engine driving through an Allison fully-automatic gearbox with automatic torque-converter lock-up on third and fourth gears. The rear axle was a double-reduction drop-centre design. The development costs of the NC project had been split between the two manufacturers; although it started out with high expectations, only eight were actually built.
Ian Allan Library

The situation generally looked more optimistic, with a healthy flow of military vehicle orders, mainly for medium-mobility and general-service trucks, about 1,500 being put into service between 1975 and 1980. Recovery appeared to have been finally achieved, with healthy profits being made by 1977.

As if to provide tangible evidence of the company's own confidence in itself, a new range of lorries (or 'trucks', as they were by now being advertised) was announced. Derived from the export model Universal, one variant was aimed at either the UK or export markets, being a 38/40-tonne tractor unit and known as the Fleetmaster. With a Cummins or Rolls-Royce engine option and Fuller transmission it was well received by the technical press of the time. The other models were the Haulmaster, with the new S10 cab, targeted at the domestic market, and the Super Haulmaster, for heavy overseas use and intended to be built in a left-hand-drive configuration. The latter featured the S90 cab and the option of a Cummins, Gardner or Rolls-Royce engine. Collectively, these new models helped the company attain a steady increase in sales, backed up with orders for a fleet of motorway gritters for the Department of Transport which had been achieved using knowledge gained whilst developing chassis for military use. A computer-controlled spare parts supply system was installed to improve efficiency still further.

◀ The first batch of 66 gritter/snowploughs was handed over to the Department of Transport in September 1978. Type designation RR27/24, these vehicles were powered by a Rolls-Royce 265 engine driving through a Foden nine-speed gearbox. Of 6x4 configuration, they had a wheelbase of 18ft and were fitted with an S85 cab with lighting modifications for their specialised role. Nylon brake-piping and anti-corrosion treatment were standard fittings. The bodywork was by Atkinson's of Clitheroe, and could carry 12 tonnes of rock salt. A rotary valve controlled by prop-shaft rotation monitored the rate of spreading. They have proved to be very successful, and later examples can be seen on the motorway network all over the UK.
John Sanderson collection

◀ The 'Super Haulmaster', intended for heavy overseas use and normally built in left-hand-drive form, was introduced in 1977. These were impressive-looking vehicles as evidenced by this six-wheel tipper. This example is fitted with a Cummins 290bhp engine and the standard S90 steel cab, although a sleeper cab was also offered. *Ian Allan Library*

Unfortunately — as so often happens in life — just as everything seemed to be going well, it all started to go wrong again. The company was actually trading profitably, but a number of crucial factors were working against it; the development costs of the new models and a fall in Middle Eastern sales, coupled with high interest charges, all combined to give a net loss figure for the year 1978/9. The storm clouds were gathering.

Recovery was certainly going to be an uphill struggle this time, although very few within the company knew how serious the situation really was. Home-market truck sales were promising, but despite encouraging noises from the bus industry relating to the NC double-decker, only eight were actually built, of which seven were put into service, one being kept as a testbed. Sadly, the company was not in a strong enough position to ride out the worldwide depression, and the financial situation was growing worse by the week.

In July 1980 the receivers were called in and, to their lasting credit, they actively tried from the outset to find a possible buyer that would take on Fodens as a going concern. Eventually, in October, a deal was completed with Paccar of Seattle, and Fodens Ltd was wound up. The name of the business was changed to Sandbach Engineering Co, trading as Foden Trucks, a subsidiary of Paccar; none of the Foden family joined the new company. Fodens had passed out of British ownership and a chapter had closed on a long and illustrious trading history.

A further unusual application for a Foden chassis is that of a horsebox. This Haulmaster, carrying the Tarmac-sponsored shire-horse team, was in Cromford, Derbyshire, in August 1988. *Author*

This NC double decker, chassis No 93742, was delivered new to West Yorkshire Passenger Transport Executive as fleet No 7250 in April 1977. It was one of seven supplied to six major fleets for evaluation in the period 1976-8. Sadly, events were to overtake this project, which did not proceed further. TUB 250R is seen here in the ownership of its subsequent operator, Aintree Coachline of Bootle. *R. Franklin / IKL*

250
AINTREE
COACHLINE
45J
Fodan
PAY AS
YOU ENTER
PLEASE
TUB 250R

This eight-wheel Haulmaster tipper was added to Seal's fleet in 1979 for use on a contract moving compacted household waste between transfer stations and tips. The 55cu yd body was built by Charlton Bros and the tipping gear was supplied by Edbro. Covering approximately 1,000 miles per week with payloads of 16½ tons, it was reported to be returning a fuel consumption of just over 7mpg from its Gardner 6LXC engine.
Ian Allan Library

The S10-cabbed Haulmaster range appeared in 1977 and carried on the Fodens tradition of producing handsome, workmanlike vehicles. Unusually, this example is a tar-sprayer, fitted with a Gardner engine and seen in Derbyshire on 18 July 1999.
Author

The Foden name survives on a range of modern trucks, still built at Elworth at the time of writing but, sadly, the news is that, by the time this book appears in print, they will be assembled elsewhere. This later history is, however, outside the scope of this book.

What we have seen is the development of a proud company; a name well respected in transport, both in the UK and overseas; a company that, more than once, was brought to the verge of extinction, but which managed to fight back; a company that, throughout its history, produced one technical innovation after another, manufacturing vehicles that were built to meet the varying needs of road-transport operators as well as those in more specialised fields; vehicles that were excellently engineered and built, and which will be remembered by operators, drivers, maintenance staff and enthusiasts alike, with affection and pride and as a product that epitomised the phrase 'the Best of British'.

K & M Hauliers of Nottingham has been a Fodens customer for many years and this sleeper-cabbed Fleetmaster tractor unit was taken into the fleet in 1979. It was fitted with a Cummins E290 engine, driving through a Fuller RT9509A gearbox to a Rockwell R180 rear axle. The bulk powder-tanker was by Carmichael and was used mainly for flour or fly ash. Travelling between Cambridge and Liverpool on contracts, it was averaging approximately 1,500 miles per week. *Ian Allan Library*

Fodens has supplied large numbers of vehicles to the British armed forces in recent years. This type of 6x6 recovery vehicle, based on a gun-tractor design, has been built from 1979. Equipped with Swedish EKA recovery equipment and both front- and rear-mounted winches of 10-ton and 25-ton capacity respectively, they are extremely capable machines. Whilst this example was built slightly outside the period covered by this volume, it symbolises, perhaps better than anything else, the ongoing Fodens tradition. *Author*

A superb working view of an eight-wheel rigid tipper — a typical Foden, and a vehicle type for which the company is justly famous. This Haulmaster was photographed at Skipton, North Yorkshire, in August 1990. *Tony Peacock*

▲

Built shortly before the takeover by Paccar was JEK 757V, an eight-wheel Haulmaster fitted with a bulk-powder tanker. The unusual colourscheme presents a striking appearance as applied to the S10 cab. *Glen McBirnie collection*